The Girl in the Purple Dress

The Girl in the Purple Dress

JO HORSLEY

StoryTerrace

CONTENTS

Foreword

Feeling as if she has little choice but to do the right thing, the young mother sitting in a bleak London bedsit is gently rocking her baby daughter to and fro in her arms. It is 1969, and society isn't yet equipped to assist single women raising children – especially mixed-race ones – born out of wedlock. With little financial means and even less support from her child's biological father or her own family miles away in Scotland, 20-year-old Isabelle Byrne knows what she must do. Sitting opposite, a social worker waits with outstretched arms to take her baby away from her. Fortunately, the social worker is patient because, try as she might, Isabelle just cannot bring herself physically to hand over her precious little girl, Anita. Each time she leans forward to pass her, it's as if her arms are on springs and they automatically recoil, pulling the child right back to her bosom. It's all too final. But handing her over for adoption is the one sacrifice that she knows she must make in order to provide a decent future for her beloved baby. There's no other way. But the price of it is painfully high. Unbearably so.

1

WHO IS THIS LITTLE GIRL?

Snuggled up in my single bed, I listen intently to the night-time story that my father is telling me. It's a fairy tale that's become so familiar, I could probably have recited it word-perfect to him.

'There you were in your little purple dress, clutching your little teddy, and I wanted to know: "Who is this lovely little girl, Anita, that's all alone? She needs a family…"'

As young as I was, I always understood that he was talking about me. I was the given-up girl left in a children's home by her red-haired Scottish mother who'd arrived in London, where she'd fallen in love and fallen pregnant by a man who didn't want to know. And my father, the good vicar, was the rescuer who still had a faded picture of that same little girl in the same purple dress that now looks pink, stuck to the inside of his wardrobe door. So here I was, living under the new name of Josephine Ruth Williams in a clergy family of nine. My father, Ray, is an Anglican vicar, and his wife, Di, is the mother of his five biological children: Rosemary, Louise, Roger, Paul and Tim. Between Paul and Tim, I came along aged 14 months old, fresh from the nursery at the Thomas Coram Foundation. So that I would have a little ally who had also arrived in a different way to the others, they also adopted my brother Ziggy. At just six weeks old, he suddenly arrived just before my mum fell pregnant with Tim, the youngest of the clan. Also like me, Ziggy was mixed race. I was half-Malaysian while he was half-Japanese. One great big happy family.

It could all have been quite different apparently had it not been for a train crash on the Bristol to Derby line that my father, at the age of 40, found himself caught up in in January 1969. Then a deputy principal of a college of education in the Midlands, he had been on his way back home from a conference. For no reason whatsoever, he decided to change seats while travelling, and soon afterwards the train crashed and derailed. Had he not done so, he would have been killed. Instead, he was unscathed. It left him feeling lucky to be alive, and it prompted a change of career. As my mother watched lunchtime TV news coverage of the serious crash knowing my father was on that same train, he was, unknowingly, about to change direction and embark on a new vocation as he helped and comforted the wounded, lighting cigarettes amidst the carnage.

Soon afterwards, he retrained as an Anglican vicar after adopting me and Ziggy through the Church Adoption Society. This wasn't before unsuccessfully attempting to adopt orphans from the Philippines and Barnardo's, though. Apparently my parents had seen an advertisement in a Sunday newspaper appealing for adoptive parents for mixed-race children and applied. After being interviewed, they were shown a series of photographs, and I stood out in my purple dress. I must have been wearing it when my parents collected me from the children's home if my father's bedtime story is to be believed. My new big sisters Ro and Louise drove down from Derby to London with my new dad on 24th April 1970 to take me home to their huge, scary redbrick house on the busy Uttoxeter Road. I hadn't really bonded with any of the staff at Coram, so the matron there told my dad (who later relayed the information to me) that I wouldn't have a problem fitting into my new life. Though initially very clingy, within weeks I was happier and more relaxed in my new surroundings, loving playing on the garden swing and in the paddling pool, according to my mum. Without any hesitation, she and my dad were ready to adopt me officially by May, and on 22nd September 1970, the adoption, complete with name change, was officially rubber-stamped at Derby County Court. Hey presto! Goodbye Anita, hello Jo!

If only it had all been that simple…

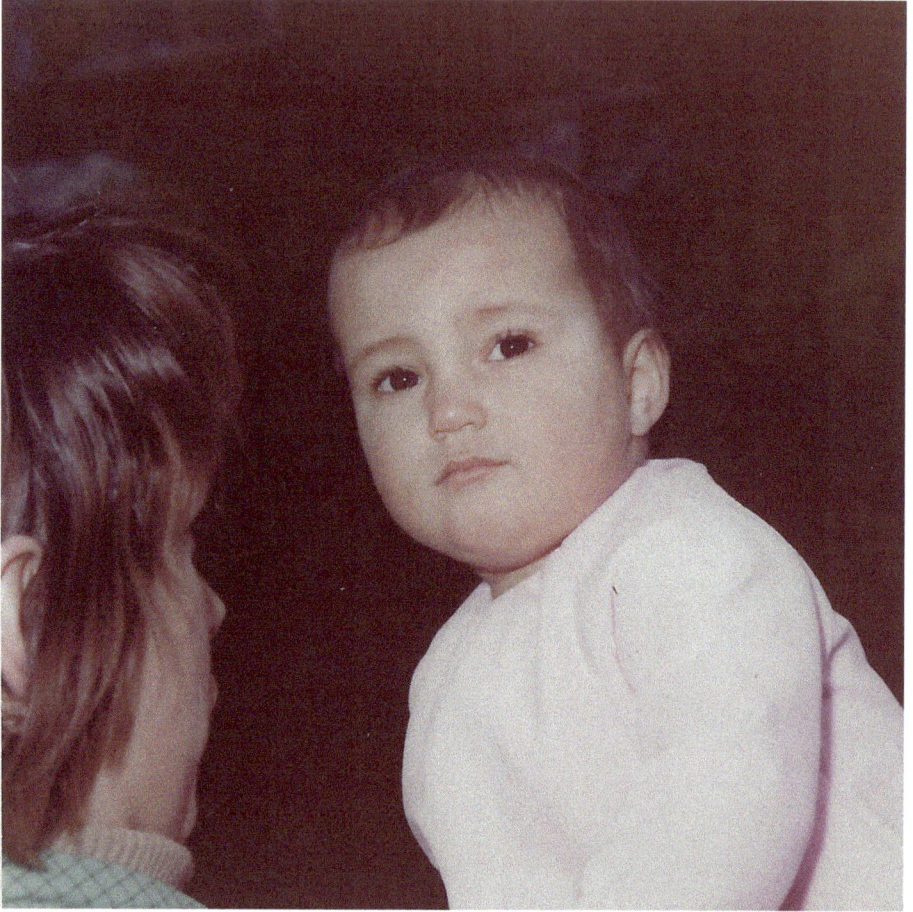

Anita (Me) 14 months @Coram

2

THE GOOD LIFE

As I'm walking down the street with my mum, a flashy car suddenly pulls up alongside us and the driver winds down the window. Through a cloud of expensive perfume, I recognise the smiling face of my new schoolfriend's very glamorous mother.

'Oh, hello Jo, we must have you to tea sometime,' she purrs.

Eyeing up the snow-white fur coat she's wearing for the school run that perfectly matches the coat of their Alaskan pet dog (and their plush home carpet, I later discover), I nodded, completely agog. This level of luxury is a world away from anything I know.

As a poor curate's family in receipt of free school meals, hand-me-down clothes and even a free holiday to Butlin's once courtesy of the church diocese, we stood out like sore thumbs in the swanky suburbs of Hertfordshire's Hadley Wood, where everyone led such glossy lives in glossy clothes in glossy homes. Yet for all that seventies sparkle – and our complete lack of it – we had a cachet about us because of my dad's standing in the church and community.

We were the 'Good Life' family as in the seventies sitcom of the same name. We kept hens to produce our eggs and even kept two goats for milk and two sheep, Flymo and Strimmer, for milk and grass cutting, as well as a donkey called Anna at one point. To our neighbours, we were regarded as different, but even they ran out of patience when we added a cockerel to our menagerie that woke them all up at the crack of dawn by crowing very loudly. Nevertheless, we were viewed as special in our little community, and as such we were exposed. Because everyone knew who we were, certain standards – especially good manners – were expected of us at all times. I imagine it's a bit like being a member of the Royal Family where you're always on public show with everyone watching your every move. At least that's how I felt. Being naturally quite a private person, I've always had a problem with that.

With a story of my own in that family, I was extra special. And I think that's even how my dad wanted me to feel when he kept repeating that bedtime story about the given-up girl. And maybe I did feel special, but it wasn't in the way he'd intended. It just made me feel very different to the others because of my background.

A sensitive little soul, I regularly cried myself to sleep at night throughout my childhood and into my teens. It was a habit that started when I was very young in that first house at Derby. Secret tears of pure sadness were wept in the privacy of my own bedroom. My parents knew nothing about them, although my mum remembers me as being 'always an unhappy child'. It's true that I was very shy and withdrawn. I had a lot of nightmares too, and in trying to escape them, I would go into my parents' bedroom in the middle of the night, desperately craving their love and connection. It was as if I had an empty well inside of me that constantly needed filling with reassurance. How much would have been enough, I've since begun to wonder? Inevitably, I was told: 'No, Jo. Go back to bed,' but eventually, they would give in and allow me to climb into their nice warm double bed with them.

As much as I felt lost in that rambling, gloomy old house, I do have some happy memories of it. I still have a clear picture in my head of sitting on the dark stairs leading up to the third-floor attic rooms that my parents rented out. One of the tenants was a lovely lady called Ros who became my godmother. She used to sit with me and read me a Ladybird book about animals. I can picture the colourful cover and the big white bear on it even now.

It is also the house where Ziggy arrived, just six weeks old, in February 1972. I honestly don't remember that much about his arrival, just the extraordinary impact he had on my life. Even though I was just short of three years older than him, we developed such a strong natural bond that we were like twins. Him the given-up boy and me the given-up girl. Two black sheep together. Our birth stories connected us and set us that bit apart from our other siblings, although as children we were also close to Tim, who was born 10 months after Ziggy arrived on 21st November 1972.

Ziggy wasn't his real name of course. It was Jeremy. He became Ziggy when he started learning to walk, doing so in zigzag lines. Originally nicknamed Zig-Zag by Mum, it was eventually shortened to Ziggy, and Ziggy he remained. I don't recall ever calling him

Jeremy – even once. As soon as he was old enough, the two of us would get up to mischief together.

There was the time we were colouring in a picture book together and I spotted a pink felt pen I wanted at the top of a tall, heavy, oak bookcase full of Bibles. So, I climbed up to get it and promptly fell down, with the bookcase toppling on me and breaking my hip. An ambulance was called, and I spent several weeks in hospital with my leg in traction. It meant that I missed the beginning of primary school, which my dad always blamed for me struggling with maths. (I am not entirely convinced that was the real reason, though!)

When I did start school, it was only for a few months, as we moved from Derby to leafy Hadley Wood soon afterwards with my dad's ministry. Happier times lay ahead for me in that new neck of the woods, it has to be said. The new vicarage at 32 Crescent East was much nicer than the house we'd left in Derby for a start. It was still huge but much less gloomy and scary. We had a lot of fun there. It was an impressive redbrick building with a grand pillared entrance attached to the pretty St Paul's Church. A long sweeping drive lay in front, and there was a big garden complete with a large horse chestnut tree that provided us with an abundance of shiny conkers to take to school and play with at break times.

On our bikes, Ziggy, Tim and I would play outdoors, disappearing for hours as we happily roamed freely round the area between the tennis courts and swings all day long before returning home for an evening meal round the big family dining table. Strangely, I don't seem to recall Mum sitting down to eat with us even though she cooked our meals. It was always up to Dad, the disciplinarian of the two, to make sure we all cleared out plates. I don't remember ever being hungry despite our meagre finances. Dinner was often a casserole or liver and onions, and I seem to recall lots of banana-flavoured Bird's Angel Delight desserts made from packets of powder mixed with milk and served with jelly. One night, I sleepwalked downstairs and into the pantry only to be caught red-handed eating ice cream straight from a tub in the freezer. Ice cream was always a treat as we avoided the carts on days out because ordering nine cones was an expensive business!

At my new primary school, despite being a bit of an outsider, I quickly made friends with children from wealthy homes, like Samantha West of the John West canned food family. I used to love going swimming in their pool, just as I loved going to friends' homes for tea or their posh birthday parties at the West Lodge Park Hotel. We never had ours there, though, and I don't remember friends coming back to our house for tea. I do recall Mum taking me and two or three friends to the cinema in Barnet to see Star Wars for one particular birthday, though – and my poor exhausted Mum falling asleep halfway through the film!

Always a bit of a diva, I liked the social side of school and have vivid memories of lifting my skirt up in the playground with the other girls and singing 'Save Your Kisses for Me' when Brotherhood of Man won the Eurovision Song Contest with it in 1976. Academically, it was a different story, and lessons are all a bit of a fog even now. I was quite good at English, and I could get my spellings right, but I couldn't seem to concentrate on anything else. Nothing ever fired me up. Not even running, even though I was the fastest in the school over a short distance. My dad tried to encourage me, bless him, cheering me on from the sidelines at races, but I just didn't have the passion for achieving anything.

It was the same at Brownies and ballet classes. There just didn't seem to be any room left in my brain for learning anything, and I fell behind.

All my end-of-year school reports said the same thing: "Josephine isn't as switched on as she could be." I came to dread the words, 'Josephine, come to my study,' that were used so regularly by my dad it became a family joke. In there, I'd get a lecture on how 'naughty little Jo' should be more like her more scholarly brothers and sisters and try harder. I always felt as if I was expected to feel grateful to them for rescuing me and giving me the life I had. To this day, I hate the word 'grateful' because grateful I never was. Thankful, yes. There is a difference, I've discovered.

Over the years, I've reflected endlessly on my past and how it's affected me. One conclusion I've reached is backed up by an amusing little snippet that my dad told me and my siblings when we were old enough to understand. Apparently, during his stint in Hadley Wood, he came across many family problems within a lot of those big houses. So, not all that glittered was as gold as it appeared. And things really aren't always what they seem.

Me & Dad

Anita (Me) 14 Months - Yes I did smile

3

REBEL, REBEL

Although I was still sobbing secretly into my pillow many nights, it was no longer every night by the time I was careering into adolescence. The reason was that I was discovering new ways of soothing my troubled soul: namely, boys and music!

As far as my studies were concerned, I suppose you could say that this was a fatal combination, but it created some amusing and fond lifelong memories.

Every time I see the former English international cricketer Phil Tufnell on TV, I have to smile remembering the time we innocently shared a quick cheeky childhood kiss by the swings. Little did he know it was his best mate Richard that I really fancied! And that was all going on while I was still in primary school. Phil T was a little bit older than I was and he had a cheeky charisma about him that appealed to girls like me with a bit of a penchant for a 'bad boy' in snakeskin trousers. Even at that tender age, the rebel in me was emerging. It's easy to see why he became a TV personality once his professional cricketing days were over!

Musically, some of my happiest memories were of freely dancing round the back living room to the Electric Light Orchestra album *Out of the Blue,* with the French doors opening wide onto the big, lush green lawn at our next house in Potters Bar. We'd moved there a year after I'd started my secondary education at Dame Alice Owen's School. Once again, it was because we were following my father's work, and he'd been moved onto becoming vicar of King Charles the Martyr Church at Potters Bar.

I'd spent the first year at my new school travelling the necessary two or three stops by train with my older brother Paul. After that, we'd all duly followed Dad in his vocational work, though I have to say that, unlike my sisters, I was sad that we had to leave lovely, posh Hadley Wood. I'd also found everything a bit scary on arrival at Dame Alice Owen's, aged 11 in September 1980, where I had continued in the same vein as I had started at Hadley Wood Primary. I was still no scholar, and those years there proved to be difficult ones.

Our new home, another grand redbrick vicarage, was only a five or 10-minute walk down the road to school for me, which gave me a bit more free time in the evenings. Not a great one for homework, I had already shown a surprising aptitude for housework. Unlike Mum, I loved cleaning and ironing and she'd even give me extra pocket for doing it. I'm still the same today, only now I have the help of a cleaner.

Back then, with so many people in our household, there was always somebody's clutter lying around – along with dog hair everywhere that was shed by our lovable pets that were less loved by me for the mess they made. My bedroom was always my sanctuary, where I could shut the rest of the world out and control my domain, free to tidy to my heart's content. I particularly loved my new bedroom at Potters Bar because of its trendy purple carpet. When I wasn't bopping around with Ziggy to our favourite ELO track 'Mr Blue Sky' downstairs, I would be up there completely alone with the door firmly shut, playing my Michael Jackson LP *Off the Wall* endlessly on a small record player perched on top of a little wooden desk with a bottle-green Formica top. Every time I placed it on the turntable, I could look out of my window overlooking the lawn and instantly recall great sunny summer days dancing in that grass.

If only I'd shown as much passion for my schoolwork… I still enjoyed English, which I put down to having a good teacher in Mr Randall who made his lessons interesting, but that was all, apart from home economics, especially cookery. In all other subjects, I was destined to lurk between the middle to bottom places of my class.

Out of the teachers' eye and earshot, I managed to find more trouble for myself. On one occasion, I nearly got myself suspended for bleaching my dark hair pale blonde in the girls' toilets at lunchtime. After secretly trying the spray-in hair lightener Sun In – which was popular in the 1980s – and emerging with bright orangey locks, it was clear that more drastic action was called for. So, with the help of a schoolfriend or two and a bottle of peroxide, I stuck my head into one of the washroom basins and let the chemicals do their job. Inevitably, there was no hiding my new bright red hair, and I got into big trouble with the headteacher. Being much darker-haired to start out with than the other girls, I stood out more than them, and I suppose the headteacher thought I was the ringleader, so I seemed to get most of the blame.

Needless to say, my dad was once again not impressed! Why couldn't I be more like my sisters and brothers who were working hard to achieve success? That didn't include Ziggy however, whose school record was similar to mine. Why that was is something I've pondered such a lot ever since.

Behind my new hair colour, though, lay a sad story that I'd kept to myself. While it was oddly acceptable for Ziggy to call me a 'little Paki' and for me to call him a 'little Jappy' in private at home, full-blown racist abuse in public was a very different and hurtful matter. This was 1980s England, and political correctness hadn't even been dreamt of by the masses. If you were different in any way, you stood out, and there was not much you could do to avoid the ignorant behaviour your differences inevitably attracted.

Walking to school one morning, I was greeted with the words "Jo Williams Paki" sprayed in white paint on the pavement between school and home. Mortified, I remember running home, fetching water and scrubbing away at it, utterly ashamed of my ethnicity. I hated being me, and I wanted to be white like my sisters and friends. I also wanted to know who my biological mother and father were. I even imagined my father might be the Malaysian-looking window cleaner that we had for a time. I used to watch Star Trek on TV and think that it was a bit like adoption. One minute you were here, and the next you were magically transported into another life. Another world.

Was it any wonder with all this going round in my head that I didn't scrape enough exam results to qualify me to enter the sixth form at Dame Alice Owen's? By now, Ro was studying to be a nurse; Louise a physiotherapist; Roger a top chef; Paul a career in marketing; and Tim was already aspiring to be a doctor. Like Ziggy, I was being left behind. A failure. What sort of future did I have?

I couldn't play the clown forever, either at home or in the classroom. The answer was to come from my father, and I will always be grateful to him for that. I was always much closer to him than I ever was to my mum, although I do have some happy memories of times with her and her own mum, my grandma, May Harwood, who was known to us as Bamam and lived in Blackpool. She was a true glamorous grandmother, and Mum was her only child (something she'd hated growing up) so we visited her frequently. These special occasions are etched in my memory, particularly the times we all piled into Bamam's Triumph Herald to view Blackpool's famous Illuminations. It was an in-joke with me and Mum that I'd have enjoyed being raised by Bamam as she had a keen interest in fashion and even had her own hat shop at one time.

Fashion wise, I will never forget Mum taking me to John Lewis in Brent Cross Shopping Centre – not somewhere we would normally shop – and buying me a pair of black jeans to wear to Samantha West's birthday party. They wouldn't have been cheap, so it was a rare treat. I can still smell the newness of the thick, dark denim today.

Like me, Ziggy needed constant love and reassurance, and he wasn't happy that I'd been singled out for such special attention. He made no secret of it; he was jealous and felt excluded. Although the two of us had our spats, we were always there for each other. Being at times a bit scared of my dad, it was always Ziggy who would take the blame if we got caught doing anything we shouldn't – like sneaking into Ro's room and fishing her discarded cigarette butts out of the wastepaper bin to light up and smoke ourselves. So sophisticated!

On a day-to-day basis, though, it was my father that I spent hours with in my teenage years. On one occasion, I even found myself accompanying him to an exorcism! (But I think it was only allowed because I was being driven somewhere by him and it was on our route.) One of his parishioners from the Cranbourne council estate in Potters Bar had complained that their garden shed or outhouse was freezing cold and haunted. I was really excited by this news. I don't know what I was expecting – a ghost hunting mission maybe. Anyway, I was hugely disappointed when we pulled up at our destination and my father promptly told me: 'You wait in the car!'

After splashing a bit of holy water around the site and saying a few prayers to bless the place, he returned but would only confirm that, yes, it was cold, when I eagerly questioned him.

More typically, we would spend time together sitting round the table discussing my complicated thoughts and feelings. Him showing the empathy necessary for (and honed by) his ministry, me choosing my words carefully.

As an adopted child, what you never want to do is to offend the parents that you've got. They were the ones who had adopted and 'saved' or 'rescued' you, so I was always quite cautious when talking a bit about my hankering to find my birth mum. But I can remember telling my dad that I would love to see her through a one-way mirror, and if I didn't like the look of her or think that she might like me, it didn't matter because I hadn't disturbed anything.

Subconsciously, I suppose I was just protecting myself from more rejection. If my birth mother had rejected me again, I don't know how I would have coped. As a result of my close relationship with my dad over the years, he'd somehow registered the abundance of love I had to give, along with my natural affinity with children. And that was to prove my ultimate saviour.

Jeremy (Ziggy) forever known as Ziggy!

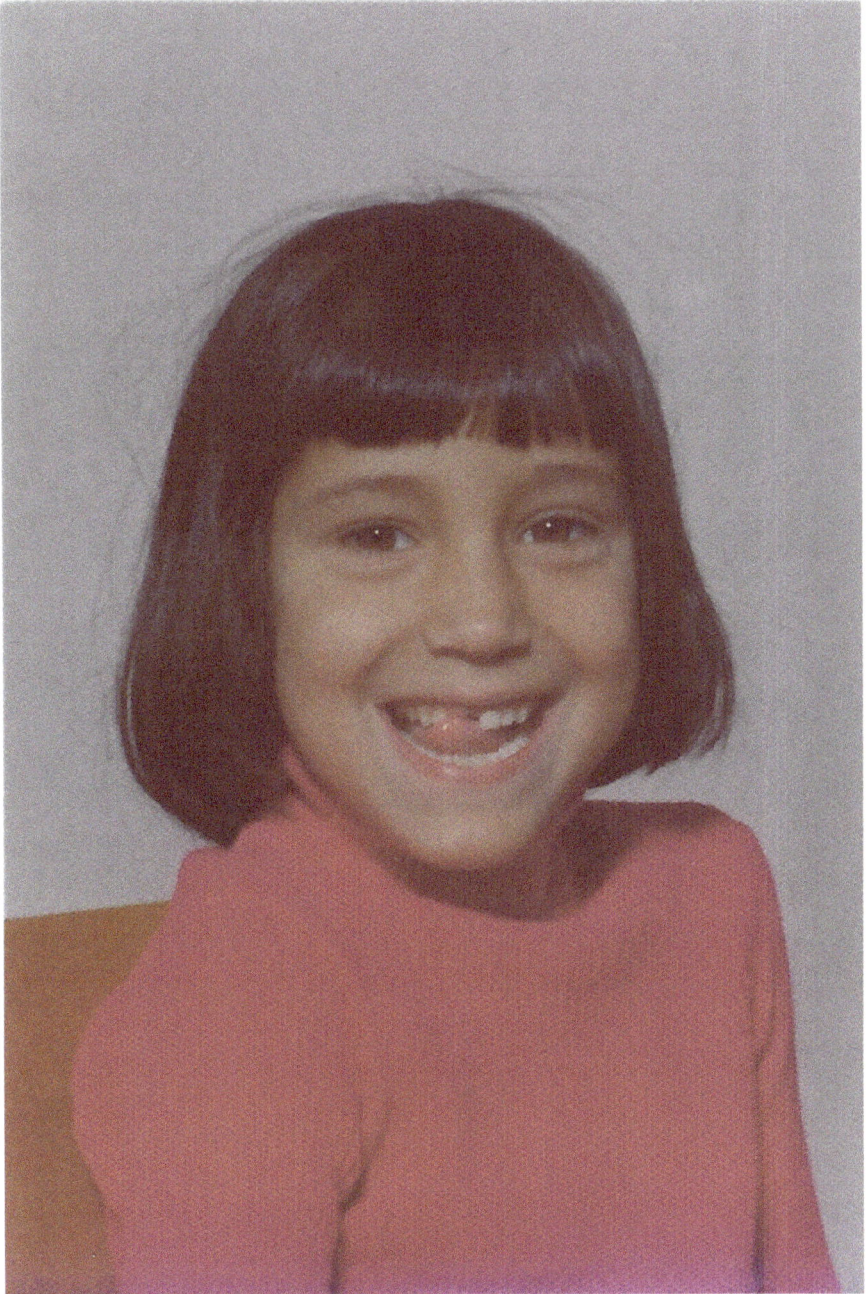

First school photo

Starting to pose for the camera!

Bridesmaid for the first time

4

SUCCESS AT LAST

As a finishing touch to the written project I've been working long and hard on, I stick the old, treasured photograph of myself in a purple dress, aged 14 months, on the A4 front cover. As I do so, a sudden and inexplicable sadness suddenly sweeps over me. Even though it's undoubtedly the right thing to do, its removal from the inside of my dad's honey-coloured wooden wardrobe door is a very poignant moment for me. It's as if the tenderness of his action in keeping it there all these years has been broken by its removal. I'm no longer there for him to see when he chooses his clean clothes every morning and, for whatever reason, I don't like the idea. It's another connection broken. Clearly, I was an extremely sensitive soul; I still am.

It had been my dad's brainwave that I should apply to go to Barnet College for two years and study for a National Nursery Examination Board (NNEB) diploma to become a qualified nursery nurse. So, I did, and despite my none-too-brilliant set of exam results – apart from a top-grade Certificate in Secondary

Education (CSE) in English that I was immensely proud of – I was accepted. A respectable great new career beckoned.

I doubt I would have ever thought of the idea myself, and I will always be thankful to my dad for doing so. Always a wise man, he encouraged me and came along with me to enrol. Growing up, people were always leaving babies at our house, which was a sort of unofficial church creche, and I loved looking after them. I felt a real connection with them. I've never lost that feeling all these years later.

I took to the course like a duck to water. The mix of practical work with more academic work suited me. I learnt about old-fashioned home economics and how to make beds properly, as well as childcare. Every Thursday and Friday, I had a placement with a lovely lady called Sally and her baby, Alice, in a beautiful Victorian house. I really liked the hands-on approach and all my tutors, especially Judy, who was very warm and motherly to her students and fun to boot. I also respected the clear edict that if you failed anything, you were booted off the course without a second chance. It was the first time I'd ever been faced with such a strict boundary rule, and even now I think there's a lot to be said for that approach. It made me buckle down anyway for the first time ever, and I passed all my exams.

Somehow, I felt safer in that college environment than I ever had in school. The tutors and the other girls were all nice, and I made some new friends. It was when I had to choose a project for my second-year coursework that my dad came up trumps again. While I was searching round for an idea, he suggested: 'How about doing a project on adoption?' I agreed, and it was decided that I should include my own story. Nobody could challenge the facts!

I must have worked hard on it because I received a really high mark for it that went towards my final exams, dictating whether I passed the course or not. I'd never had such a high mark for anything I'd ever done before. To my delight, I passed my diploma course with flying colours, and I made my dad very proud of me in the process.

Glad to have made him proud, I was equally proud of myself. It was a good feeling, though it was a double-edged sword. My own life story had finally made me successful!

Rummaging through some old papers recently, I found an old reference from my tutor written by her when I was approached by an independent boys' prep school about a vacant post there. It reads as follows:

> To whom it may concern,
>
> I was Josephine Williams' health tutor at Barnet College, while she was studying for her N.N.E.B. During her time at college, she worked hard and conscientiously at her coursework as well as at her college work. I observed her in practical work situations, in a nursery, in a school and with a family of three young children. She related well to both staff and children, was punctual and showed initiative in practical situations. Josephine is a pleasant, cheerful young lady, and I feel sure she will fit in well in a working situation with young children.

Judy Pewsey SRN

Praise indeed! It turns out that all I really needed throughout those years spent in education was the right sort of encouragement and environment. Onwards and upwards.

First secondary school photo, still smiling just!

5

WORKING HARD AND PLAYING HARD

As focussed as I was at college, my family and personal life remained incredibly up and down during those same teenage years. To be honest, a lot of it is so incredibly blurry, maybe I've blocked it out.

What I do clearly remember though is one particular nasty spat with Ziggy, who sadly never went on to find his vocational niche in the way that I had. It was a real bust-up that I'll never forget, over his girlfriend creating a mess in the kitchen by leaving her riding boots in the sink. I reacted, even though I probably shouldn't have done.

We could be equally fiery when roused, and soon Ziggy was pulling my hair out by the roots really hard. It hurt, and I hit back at him just in time for Mum to walk into the kitchen and catch me. Pointing her finger straight in my direction, she told me unequivocally: 'Get out.'

I didn't need telling twice, and a period of sofa surfing followed. The years between 16 and 18 had not been my finest in every aspect except college, and I think she was probably just fed up with the messes I had got myself into – including a 'relationship', if you can really call it that, with an older man that had started even before I was 16. He'd seen me in my school uniform and offered me a lift in his flashy sports car. He was a bit of a father figure to me, but soon enough our 'relationship' was far from any normal father and daughter one…

I had a key to his beautiful house and could come and go as I pleased, making use of his round bath or well-stocked bar. I even took my friends there. He repeatedly took me to nice places, wining and dining me while showering me with expensive gifts: jewellery, a leather jacket, flashy shoes and clothes. To avoid raising suspicion at home, I kept them at his house. Nevertheless, my dad's suspicions were raised when he discovered a love letter from him and a pack of contraceptive pills. He got one of the church people to watch where I was going, and once they followed me to the phone box where I'd gone to call him.

I think both Mum and Dad knew exactly what was going on. I can't pretend that I was an angel, but looking back, he groomed me. It was illegal as I was under 16. I was a victim struggling with low self-esteem and ripe for the taking. When he eventually dropped me like a hot potato, telling me: 'We've come to our end,' as soon as another woman came along, I felt bitter and hurt. It was yet another rejection and had probably alienated me further from my disapproving family.

Although I had repeatedly threatened: 'The day I am 18, I am out of here,' I hadn't got as far as making any plans. There was a lot of to-ing and fro-ing at friends' homes. Despite letters arriving from my dad begging me to return home, I realised my relationship with Ziggy was too explosive for me to be there at the time. It's all a bit of a muddle.

After that nasty little episode with the older predator, I found myself a couple of more suitable boyfriends. The first, Gary (not his real name), was a DJ when he wasn't working at his day job fixing amusement arcade slot machines. He lived locally and he was lovely – really nice. His mum was lovely too. I remember she bought me a lovely glass penguin for my 18th birthday, which was celebrated with a party thrown by my parents for me in the church hall. The local policeman and his wife manned the bar just in case things got out of hand.

As ever, there had to be a scene with my family, and this time it was caused by me wearing a backless black dress that the groomer had previously bought for me. 'You're not wearing that!' was my father's response when he saw it, and to be fair, he had a point. The style was much too old for me. My mum let her anger show afterwards, and there was another big fight.

My relationship with Gary didn't last very long, and I moved on to Mark (not his real name), who was the brother of one of my college friends, Mandy (not her real name). He was very shy and told me that from his bedroom window, he used to watch my calf muscles twitching in my little heels as I was walking home from college. Too shy to ask me out for ages, we did eventually get together, and when things were too bad at home, I ended up living at his house for about a year, sleeping in the little piano room downstairs.

I think a lot of people – including my parents, who were keen to see me settle down – thought we'd marry. He was a nice, very clever boy from a good family, but that wasn't meant to be our fate. We did stay together for around five years, though, and we shared a lot of fun during that time. We even took out a joint mortgage on a flat in Welwyn Garden City.

After I'd graduated, I took a live-in nanny job with a nice Jewish family in Hemel Hempstead, but it wasn't really the right post for me as the mum was permanently around and didn't really need my input. I was bored because I wasn't being challenged, and I felt quite lonely. After a few months or so, I quit and ended up working in a video rental shop with Mark. And what a ball we had!

One of our regular customers was the pop singer Stedman Pearson from the group Five Star, who Mark got to know quite well because of their shared interest in films. One minute he was inviting us out for a drink in the pub, and the next we were on our way to Los Angeles, Beverly Hills, Disneyland and Gstaad, with him footing much of the bill. He was never anything but a proper gentleman, and we were all just good mates. Stedman was just richer, a bit older and much more successful than we were. Some of those memories will stay with me forever – like the time I had a baseball cap on and was mistaken for Janet Jackson by some of his fans. My own 15 minutes of fame!

Once, when we were being chauffeured round Gstaad, eating posh chocolates, I told him: 'I want to be famous like you, Sted,' but he replied wisely: 'No Jo, you couldn't handle it. You are wonderful, but you wouldn't cope.' Obviously, he had sensed my vulnerabilities.

Sted also asked me about my birth mum, and I told him: 'My mum must have been such a strong person to give me up. I don't believe she gave me up easily.' He turned round and in a serious voice said: 'You are growing into being such a lovely, intelligent woman, Jo. I am so proud of who you are becoming.' That was one of the nicest things I think anybody had ever said to me until then, and I will never forget it.

I adored Sted. He was so humble despite all his success. He came to visit us in our flat that had been bought on a dodgy mortgage deal, and he even stayed at Mark's parents' house when they were away on holiday. By the time I was 20, though, I was ready to start my nursery nursing career properly, and I was offered a post at Lochinver House School after being recommended for it – a real boost to my self-esteem. I was employed as a nursery nurse and school nurse there for around 10 years. Those years were to shape my future yet again.

As I was changing and evolving all the time, it also meant that I was ready to move on from Mark by then. Sadly, he wasn't, and it was a very difficult time. I felt terrible, but I knew that it was time for us to split up.

Sensibly, we kept the flat and rented it out. I moved into digs above the school, which were in a sort of castle turret. I felt like a princess up there, and despite the building's dark, spooky ambience, I was never scared – unlike Ziggy when he came to visit. 'How do you live here?' he asked, aghast. But then, I'd always harboured secret dreams of meeting a prince. And that wasn't to happen for a few years to come. Before then, in the best fairy tale tradition, I had to kiss a few frogs first…

Growing up…

6

A MARRIAGE MADE IN HEAVEN?

Holding onto Dad's arm, I am walking misty-eyed down the aisle of his old church, King Charles the Martyr. There waiting at the top of it is my tall, handsome husband-to-be, Edward (not his real name). Solemnly standing at the altar ready to marry us is my mum, who has recently been ordained and is fully gowned up for the job. It's an emotional family affair all right, but it's one that, in my heart of hearts, I know should not be happening. Not this day or any other. As such, the tears misting my eyes are not ones of pure joy but despair.

So desperate was I to find a happy fairy tale ending to my troubled life story, I fell into a marriage that didn't even last long enough for me to bother changing my name on my chequebook. And, as ever, I only had myself to blame.

As soon as I had clapped eyes on Ed, I'd been drawn to him and quite shamelessly had pursued him. He had arrived at Lochinver as a science teacher and there was an almost immediate spark between us. As my good friend and colleague Ros said after spotting us chatting in the corridor: 'The chemistry was there!' Even from a distance, she could sense the powerful attraction between us. My parents liked him and quickly had him marked down as good husband material – the one to take me off their hands once and for all. 'He's just like my father!' enthused my mum, clearly delighted that I'd landed myself such a catch.

Unfortunately for them, it didn't work out like that. It was doomed from the start. Despite the long white dress, flowers and vows, deep down, I didn't want to be marrying this man and was only doing it to please my parents. There was an awful lot of pressure on me.

No sooner had the wedding cake been cut than we were heading for the rocks. It probably didn't help our newly wedded life that after a short honeymoon in Paris, we'd moved into my parents' home with them. I don't think Ed was ever comfortable there, and neither was I. Underneath it all, I don't think I ever really trusted Ed, to be honest. Ros had once pointed out that I was very in tune with my own feelings – unlike a lot of people – so maybe I am naturally intuitive. Perhaps it's a trait I've inherited from my biological mother. Or father? How would I know? Whichever, things came to a head with Ed within months of our wedding when I discovered that he had been in touch with an old girlfriend just before he had proposed to me. Time to move on. Again. Mum nearly died when I returned home (we were both living in Lochinver by now) to tell her that I was leaving Ed. A more positive response came from the headmaster, Patrick, when I went in to explain the situation. 'One thing we've always known about you and loved about you, Jo, is your unpredictability!' he told me. 'We don't know what you'll do next.'

Throughout the 10 years or so I worked at Lochinver, Patrick and his wife, Claire, who I got to know when making cricket and rugby teas, were nothing but kind to me. They understood me and were like surrogate parents. Their two children, Harriet and Matthew, were lovely too, and I did wonder what I'd have turned out like if they'd been my parents. I've since learnt that 'what ifs?' don't get you anywhere. There are no parallel lives. 'No going back' was rapidly becoming my go-to mantra.

Me & Sted glamorous times in Geneva

Thoughtful in Geneva

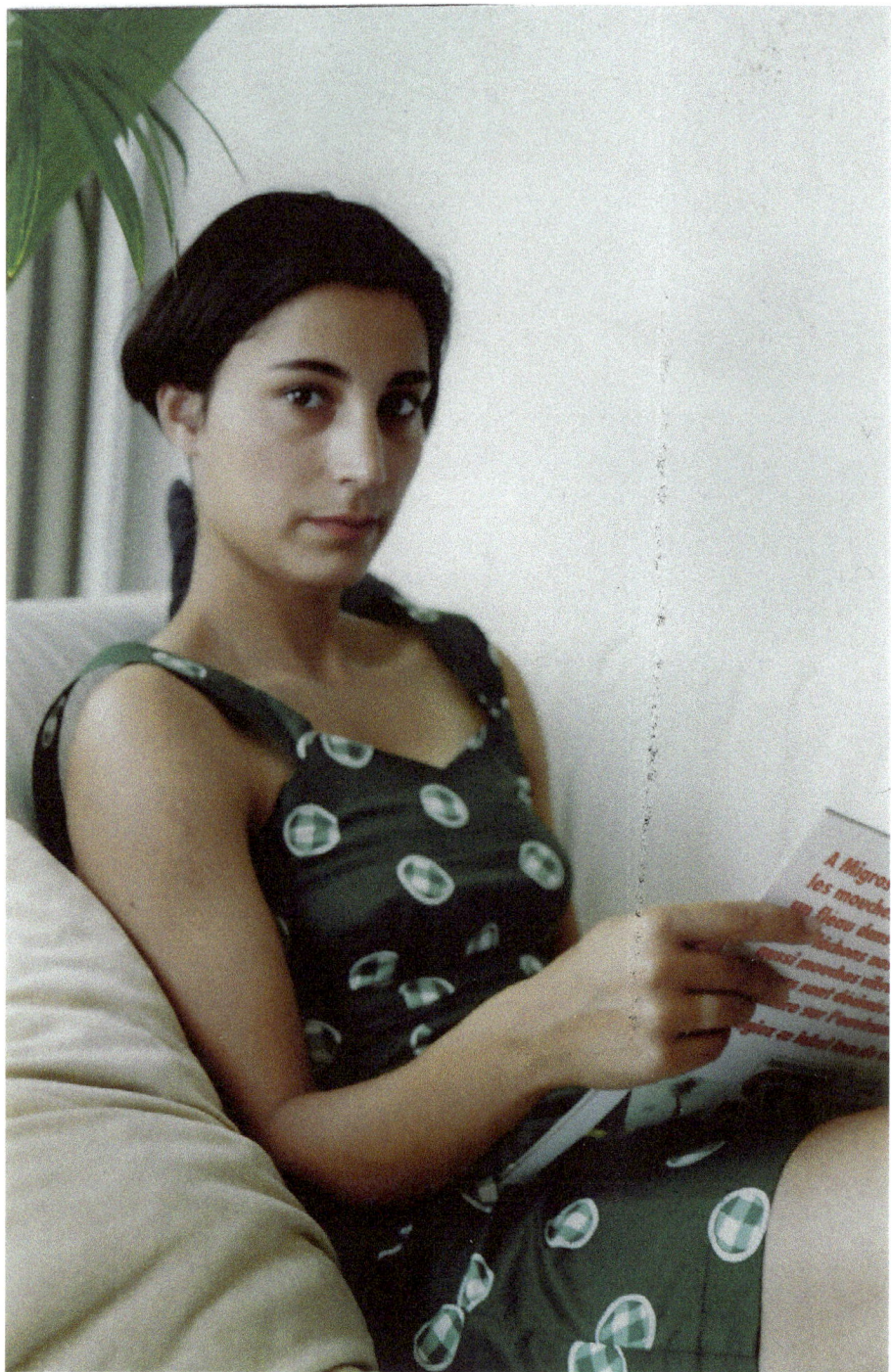

Posing for the camera, again!

7

MY GIFT FROM GOD

Skipping and dancing into the kitchen at my parents' seafront holiday home in Eastbourne, I have an important announcement to make: 'This is the happiest day of my life! I'm pregnant! I'm going to have a baby!' To me, it was the ultimate special thing that could happen – the best feeling in the world. Fortunately, my new boyfriend, Doug, is happy too, even though he's too shellshocked to actually dance and cheer along with me, as my brother Roger and sister-in-law Shona do.

It was summer 1998, and I was happily divorced from Ed. As it turned out, the messy ending of our marriage resulted in him leaving his job and moving out. I stayed put and danced away the heartache of a failed marriage, alone in my room, to the sound of David Bowie, U2 and The Beatles.

Then along came Guillaume, a French student teacher who, like me, was alone. Purely as friends, we had a lot of fun hanging about together in The Builders Arms pub across the road, him teaching me the difference between savoury and sweet crepes, and driving round in the white Renault automatic car I'd treated myself to.

Once Guillaume was back in France and I was a bit more cheered up, Doug arrived to teach maths and geography at Lochinver. He was the complete opposite to Ed in looks, being much shorter and stockier. Yet, we hit it off and spent many a happy hour downing a few drinks together. It transpired that we were destined to spend the next five years together, and we created the happiest, best thing I've ever had in my life…

I wasn't trying to get pregnant but, admittedly, I was quite clearly not not trying when we visited my parents' holiday home on Eastbourne seafront. I am pretty sure that's where I conceived the baby I was desperately yearning for, and it is definitely the place where my pregnancy was confirmed on a later weekend visit with Roger and Shona.

After mentioning to Shona that I was feeling really irritable and was going to the loo a lot, she declared: 'I think you need to get a pregnancy test.' Totally naive, my reaction was: 'Whaaat?' She went out and bought two, which I used straightaway before returning, utterly euphoric, into the kitchen. Our baby was very much wanted from the word go. Even if I'd had to go it alone or live in a tent, there was nothing that was ever going to stop me from having this baby, and keeping her.

When Emily Rose Baxter was born, two weeks early, at Barnet Hospital weighing 5lb 15oz on 14th April 1999, it was no surprise to me. Despite the confidence of the Irish midwife who had earlier declared that I was having a boy 'for sure, for sure' after detecting a quick heartbeat, I knew, without a shadow of a doubt, that I was having a little girl. I knew that she would be fair-haired and blue-eyed – not dark like me. And I knew that her name would be Emily after my father's mother as I'd promised him years beforehand. I'd never been more certain of anything in my life. It was as if God had told me so.

Within days of discovering that I was pregnant, I had gone along to a hot air balloon show in Trent Park, where I'd talked to my unborn daughter about what I was seeing. Even then, I could feel a strong connection to my tiny unborn baby, and it was a wonderful feeling.

As Emily had been in the breach position, and efforts to turn her had failed, I had to have an elective caesarean section, which meant that, thankfully, I was awake for the whole experience. Ever the joker, I remember asking the doctor giving me the epidural injection in my spine: 'Can you give me a pedicure while you're down there?'

As soon as she was scooped out of me, Emily was whisked off to a far corner of the operating theatre as she hadn't cried. 'Is she all right?' I anxiously asked my mum, who as always was around for the big life occasions. Reassuring me that all was fine, she added: 'She's got blue eyes and blonde hair.' So, I had been right all along!

As soon as she cried and the medics were satisfied that she was fine, she was brought straight back to me. And like a little sparrow, she looked up at me with those blue eyes as if to say: 'There you are, Mum! I know you've had a glass of wine and a cigarette or two during pregnancy. I know you've been a monkey!' Yet, without any judgement, she accepted me, flaws and all – unconditionally. In return, I held her tightly, loving her so much that I just wanted to wrap her in cotton wool and never let her go. I never wanted anything bad that had happened to me to happen to her. Maybe this bizarre new feeling was what I'd been craving all along. My own little girl. My Em. My gift from God.

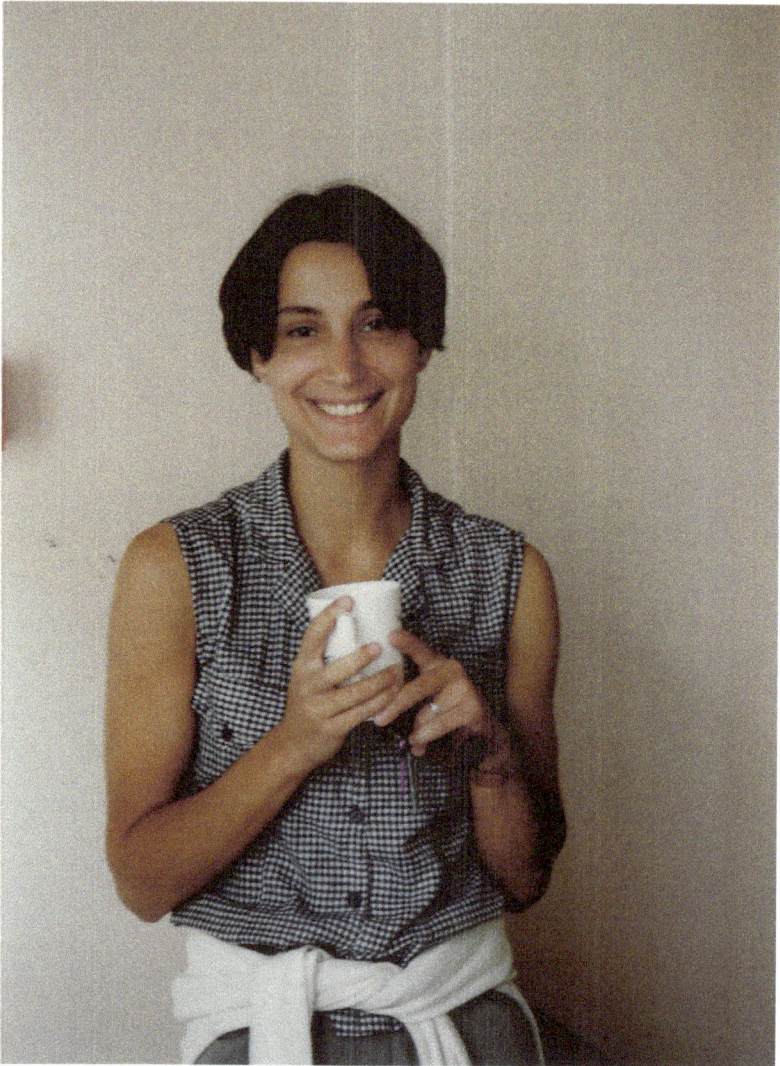

Lochinver Days

8

TROUBLE UP NORTH

One of the more sensible decisions that I've made in my life was to buy out Mark's share of the little flat in Welwyn Garden City and rent it out. It was to there that the three of us retreated to begin family life.

Although I was every bit as much in love with Em as the moment I first saw her, I can vividly remember feeling quite lonely during the long days when Doug was at work at Lochinver. Mum's visits were rare, and Doug's mum, Carol, who'd been such a great support in the early days, lived too far away in Loughborough to be a regular visitor. When we saw her and her late husband, John, they both spoilt Em something rotten. Shona and Ro popped in when they could, but I seemed to spend an awful lot of hours alone with my new baby daughter.

Strangely, I hadn't thought too much about my biological mother after becoming a mum myself. I know that a lot of adopted women ask themselves 'Why?' at that point, including the woman in the next bed to me at the hospital. I think I just felt numb. It took more than a whole decade and a sudden tragic death, not a birth, for those feelings to surface…

By 2003, Doug had been diagnosed with the inflammatory disease sarcoidosis, which affects multiple organs in the body. Quite poorly, he'd been in and out of hospital for some time, and I didn't deal very well with the situation. Once recovered, it left him with itchy feet, and he wanted us to leave Welwyn Garden City to move north to Kendal. He had been at teacher training college there and had always vowed to return to live in the area one day.

It was a huge wrench for me. I'd gone back to work at Lochinver, and Em was settled at playgroup with her childminder. Yet Em, Doug and I were a unit, even though he never made any moves to marry me. Had he asked, I would have said yes, but Doug was Doug. As my dad said, he was so laid back, he was horizontal.

Despite giving up my good job without any guarantee of another, I agreed to go and sobbed my heart out leaving Lochinver, where I had progressed from classroom assistant and school nurse to deputising for matron. It would have been cruel to deny Doug his dream, and it was a fresh start filled with hope. I've always loved fresh starts.

I had a glowing reference from Patrick, the headmaster, to help me find similar employment up in the South Lakes, so with fingers firmly crossed, I took a gamble.

On the hottest day of the summer, we packed up all our possessions in a white hire van, and Doug drove us up north to Kendal, where we'd rented a house using some of the proceeds of the Welwyn Garden City flat sale to tide us over. It didn't take long for me to realise that the decision had been a rash one and an absolute disaster for all of us.

I'd left behind everyone and everything I knew – all my friends, family and colleagues. Doug never found a teaching job, and the pressure was on me to earn money to fund our new life. So, to pay the bills and avoid any more sleepless nights worrying how we'd manage financially, I took a part-time job in the trendy women's clothes shop Monsoon, leaving Em in Doug's care until she started school. She was always close to her dad, and he in turn adored her.

On the plus side, I made lots of lovely new girlfriends who worked with me at Monsoon and didn't make me feel quite such an outsider in this strange part of the world. They'd invite me on nights out, and of course, I had stacks of nice clothes to wear that had been bought with my generous staff discount.

Life at home, though, wasn't getting any better, and the cracks in our relationship were really starting to show. Work still eluded Doug, and I resented being the sole breadwinner. For starters, I'd never been good with money myself, and I didn't like the responsibility being put on me. If things didn't improve quickly, I could see how Em's home was soon not going to be a happy home. Things came to a bit of a head on a trip to see my parents who'd invited me down soon after I'd spilled all my woes on the phone to them. Doug wasn't interested in coming with me, and I was distraught to find myself stuck in traffic for hours on end, often taking wrong turns, which meant the journey took twice as long as it should have done. It woke me up to the fact that Doug wasn't really by my side in any of this new life, and I wanted to go back to my old life.

Perilously close to a breakdown, tears streamed down my face as I battled with the fears and thoughts buzzing round my frazzled brain. And then, I was brought back to earth by a little voice in the back seat just audible above the sound of the nursery rhymes playing on a loop in the CD player. My precious little Em, sensing her mother's despair, was reassuring me: 'Don't worry, Mummy.' For her sake and mine, I knew in that instant that I had to pull myself together – keep going forward.

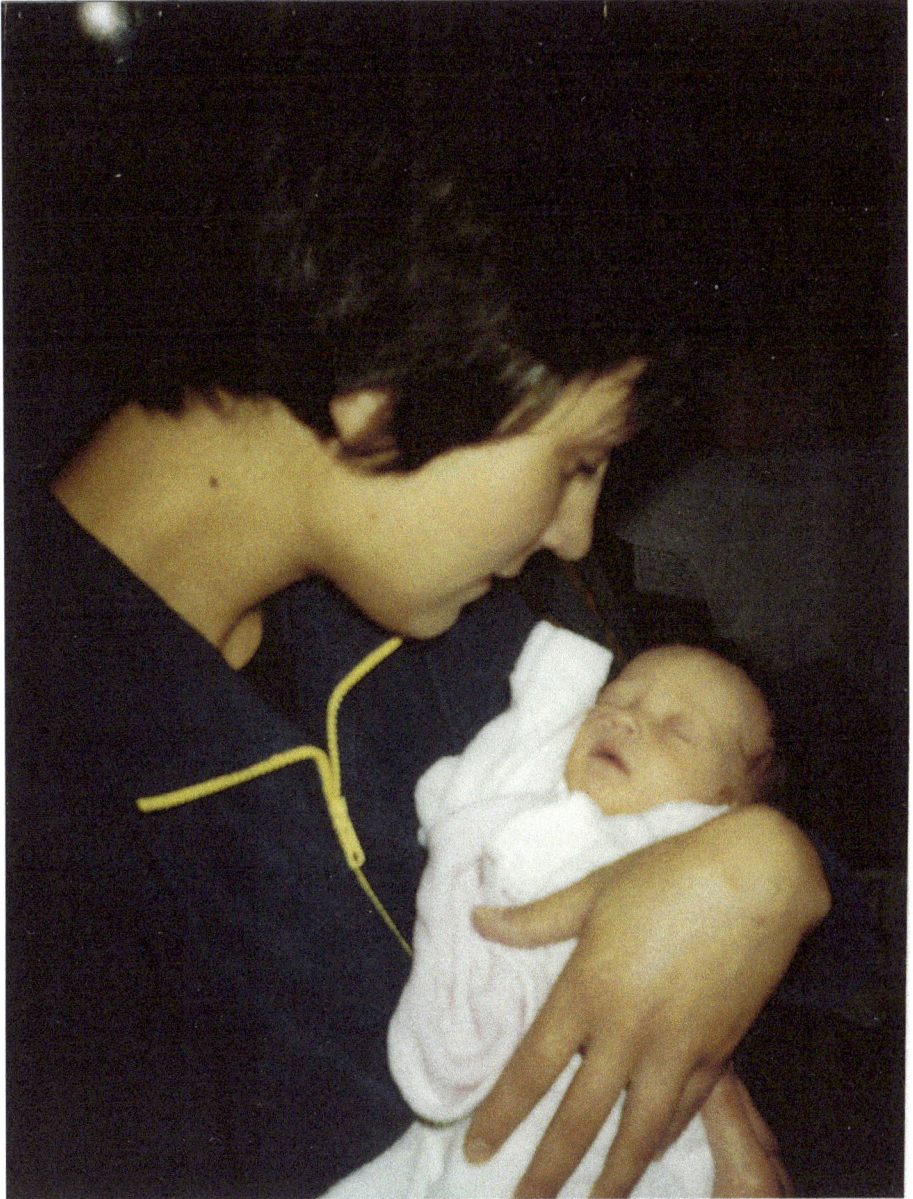

Most precious bundle Emily 1999

A pensive thoughtful Em Ullswater

Me aged two

with my mum

Mum & Daughter photographed by Ziggy

9

THE PRINCE AND THE SHOPGIRL

The tall man in the leather jacket catches my eye the moment he walks through the door of Monsoon one Saturday afternoon late in 2004. Male customers are a bit of a rarity anyway, and this one looks particularly striking. But he looks as if he's carrying the weight of the world on his shoulders. Poor chap.

To my surprise, he ignores my two younger, far more glamorous colleagues and makes a beeline straight for me. When I questioned him later on this, he said I had a light around me, like an aura, which drew him in.

'Hello. Can I have some assistance, please?' he asks while pointing a finger firmly in my direction. Taking in his green eyes and chiselled features, I think: 'Wow! He's handsome!'

Suddenly, my heart's pumping, and I feel completely overwhelmed and panicky as he explains that he needs help buying dresses for the two daughters he'd brought with him.

It was his brother's wedding, and the girls – eight-year-old Freya and five-year-old Lauren – needed suitable outfits to wear. I busy myself sorting them out, running from the stockroom to the fitting room, but all the while, I can feel a sense of something strange. Eventually, we all agree on a blue velvet dress and a soft green chiffon one that are later approved and admired by the girls' grandparents. He pays and turns to go, looking a bit happier than when he came in.

'He was nice, wasn't he?' I comment to my colleagues as I watch him walk back out of the door, but they're completely oblivious to what I'm talking about. Oh, well. I compose myself for the next customer, unnerved by the interlude but not expecting to see him again in a million years. He hadn't even so much as glanced back in my direction after achieving what he'd come in for.

Little did I know that while I was experiencing all those odd feelings, so was he… And a few days later, in he walked again. *Oh, what now?* I wondered as my heartbeat quickened again and my stomach lurched. I nervously started tidying the accessories counter, which was where he found me. 'Hello,' he smiled. 'Hello! I hope everything was okay with your daughters' dresses?' I replied. 'Oh, yes,' he reassured me. 'I just wanted to come in and say thank you for such great customer service.'

Then came the million-dollar question: 'How would you feel if I asked you to come out for dinner?' Knocked completely off-kilter, I stuttered: 'Well, yes,' then paused and added: 'But no… ' Going on to explain that I already had a partner and a young daughter of my own, he suggested: 'Oh, maybe just a cuppa, then?'

Flustered, I explained that it was my turn to take up my shift on the till, and he followed me over. Handing me his business card, which revealed his name as Simon Horsley, he smiled and said: 'If your circumstances change…'

Then, he turned on his heel and disappeared once more, leaving me struggling with a gamut of emotions. Yes, I was really flattered and excited by his attention. But I was also equally dismayed. There's no doubt that things were not right between Doug and me, but I am naturally a very loyal person, and the last thing I was looking for was another man. I had enough problems already without any more complications. Em was only five years old, and the one thing I wanted above anything else for her was something I felt I never had: total stability and security. I owed her that much. She didn't need this, and neither did I. Or did I?

So, confused, I phoned an old, trusted friend for reassurance, and she advised: 'I think you'd better keep hold of that card, Jo.'

As it happened, I didn't need to because four or five days later, he was back in the shop handing me another piece of paper, saying, 'I've written this for you.' All his cool allure disappeared as he revealed his hand in a poem, which was to be the first of many I would receive.

Completely bemused, I turned to my manager for advice this time, and she suggested: 'Why not just meet him for a cuppa?' So, the next time he appeared out of nowhere, I agreed to meet him for a coffee in Costa the next day.

There, sitting opposite him, I began to think he was a bit full-on. With me not being used to that level of attention, it was a bittersweet experience. I felt nervous but excited and fearful. How on earth was this going to come to anything? But as we chatted, all my worries melted away momentarily. Bizarrely, it was as if everybody around us had dispersed and we were in this place alone together. He explained that he was separated and almost divorced from his wife. I told him about my own situation. He invited me out to dinner at the end of the coffee, and I said, sadly: 'I just don't think I can.' Not that I wasn't sorely tempted.

Another chat with my boss persuaded me to call him up and tell him: 'I can't do this.' A hard one to shake off, he replied: 'At least can we be friends?' and I agreed.

Back at home, Doug had started asking questions, wanting to know if I was okay. Obviously, he was sensing that something was going on with me. It was while lying in the bath that I decided to get dressed, go out and call Simon from a phone box down the road. We agreed to meet at a brewery bar in Kendal, 40 minutes later, which we did, and from there he drove me out to a pub in Windermere. I hated lying as I'd told Doug I was going out with the girls from Monsoon.

Feeling extremely nervous about it all, I was very surprised when Simon sat down with a drink and admitted that he was nervous too. After I'd downed a few glasses of white wine to ease my nerves, he drove me home and leaned over in the car to kiss me goodnight. I didn't have a clue how on earth this was all going to pan out, but there was no point pretending anymore.

The rest, as they say, is history. For the record, splitting up with Doug and causing heartache for Em is not something I am proud of, but I really didn't feel that I had any choice in what was happening. Even my own dad told me, without even meeting

Simon, 'I'm going to encourage you to go for this, Jo. I think it's right for you.' Like me, he knew that I had no real future with Doug. Our whole relationship had been based on us going down to the pub and having a laugh from the start. Sadly, I needed more than that now and I didn't feel it was a strong enough foundation for family life.

Splitting up wasn't easy. It never is, and there were a few nasty scenes. Doug found poetry that Simon had written to me and confronted me. I confessed, and he promised to change. But I knew deep down that he wouldn't. Obviously, he became hurt and angry, and one day I returned home from work to find all my clothes and belongings strewn across the front lawn. He'd thrown them out, and I knew it was time to go.

The situation at home was escalating and would only get worse. But of course, there was Emily to consider in the middle of all this. Eventually, after much coming and going, just before Christmas, Simon rented a little terraced house where I could live with Em. I'll never forget the Christmas Day night: the two of us walked in the snow and ice from one end of Kendal to the other, pulling Em's little trolley suitcase with some of her clothes and toys. The only furniture we had in there was a mattress along with some bedding, but the relief of having our own four walls was enormous. I knew that Simon would help me sort everything in time.

The guilt of it all was killing me. I knew I'd really hurt Doug and Em, and the sight of her waving goodbye to her daddy through the window when he turned up at the rental house out of the blue was heartbreaking. Friends who knew the story of how Simon and I got together would say 'How romantic,' but it wasn't all moonlight and roses by any stretch. We had three children to consider in all this. Somehow, we got through the first year. We introduced Em to Freya and Laura on a farm visit, and very gradually, the worst of the storm began to blow over; things became a little easier.

When Simon suggested a walk after his 41st birthday dinner on 30th June 2005 as it was such a lovely evening, my initial response was to moan. In my best pink strappy Monsoon dress and sparkly flip flops, I complained: 'I can't walk in these… ' Insistent, he cajoled me, saying: 'Come on. I want you to see the views and the stars.'

Naively, I followed him up the steps of Kendal Castle, and when we reached the top, he promptly fell down on one knee. 'Will you marry me?' he grinned. I loved the question so much that I asked him to repeat it before answering: 'Yes!' I was elated but also in a state of shock. 'Why did you bring me to the castle to propose?' I wanted to know. Grinning from ear to ear, he told me: 'You're my princess.' One thing I knew for absolute certain: Simon was my prince all right.

First Christmas in Kendal

10

OUR BIG DAY

To the romantic sound of George Michael's lyrics, 'I think you're amazing,' I am swishing down the staircase at Windermere's Langdale Chase Hotel in my posh, strapless, silk wedding dress, clutching a bouquet of white roses and eucalyptus.

It's Bonfire Night, 5th November 2006, and more than a year since Simon proposed. A lot has settled down by then. Though ever loyal to her daddy, Em has really warmed to Simon, and although I wouldn't win any stepmother of the year awards, I was doing my best to get along with Freya and Laura, who sadly couldn't be with us on our big day.

Happily, everyone else who was important to us is here, and we've taken over the entire hotel for the weekend to accommodate our 50 or 60 guests. Ziggy, who's volunteered to take our wedding photos with the help of his old friend Russ, is constantly by my side snapping away, and Emily looks divine in her navy velvet Monsoon bridesmaid dress. Happy day!

My other family members are all here but purely in a guest capacity. It's important to me that this time Mum and Dad aren't leading proceedings on this occasion and are merely enjoying it along with Simon's parents, relatives and friends.

As we make our vows in the presence of two female registrars, Simon slips a yellow-gold wedding band onto my finger that perfectly complements the simple diamond solitaire engagement ring we chose together from H. Hogarth jewellers. His sister, Lorna, plays the saxophone beautifully to mark the end of the ceremony.

'You're marrying James Bond!' Ziggy jokes, and I laugh. It's such a treasured memory for me now… Ziggy and I were still so close at that point. He liked Simon, and he was happy for me.

For his part, Ziggy was as happy that day as it was possible for him to be. He used to say to me: 'Everyone has their demons, Jo.' I think Ziggy had a lot of demons.

Despite his many talents, he had never really found his path through life. A really good-looking guy, he could also put his hand to most things artistically. He'd had a few extra parts in big TV dramas like *EastEnders*, *London's Burning* and *Only Fools and Horses*. He was a really good cook and a brilliant artist. Even when he was in prison, he produced some great photos and one was actually hung up at a function at the Tate Gallery in London.

I like to think that I never turned my back on him in whatever circumstances he found himself. I visited him in prison, where he spent two years after being sentenced over an altercation with his girlfriend, and I took Em with me once when she was only little, but

I did regret doing that. She hadn't a clue what was going on, and I shouldn't have put her in that position.

When Ziggy was living rough on the streets in London's West End, I visited him after work to give him money or bring food. It used to break my heart, especially if his mind was away with the fairies after sniffing glue. I remember looking at him once and sobbing to see him in those circumstances. I just wanted to scoop him up and take him home, but he would adamantly tell me: 'Go now, Jo…'

I am also grateful for the kindness of strangers. Every time I see the actor Nigel Havers in anything on TV, I bless myself and say, 'Thank you, Nigel.' When he was going in and out of the theatre where he was performing, he would pass Ziggy sitting outside in a cardboard box and would always take the time to speak to him. He probably gave him money too. Ziggy even met Princess Di once, when she came back stage after one acting role in Sadler's Wells Theatre.

At other better times, Ziggy was in and out of all sorts of jobs. He even worked at a funeral director's and used to scare us by telling us how dead bodies would still let off air. Ziggy was never afraid of death and, if anything, he seemed to have a morbid fascination with it. With Ziggy, you just could never tell what he would do from one day to the next. He was full of ideas and plans for something different every week.

But on our big day, he just relaxed into the occasion along with everyone else. It was very special to have him there, and he was the life and soul of the party. He had a project to keep him occupied and was even on the verge of making a good career as a photographer.

I'll never forget him describing the breathtaking view from the window of his room at Langdale Chase. He spoke so eloquently and emotionally about how calming the reflection of the perfect moon on Lake Windermere was and how he felt at such peace with himself that he would have been happy to die there. Again, there was that morbid fascination coming through…

Nothing and nobody could spoil my big day or, as I really should say, my big weekend. Many of our guests had arrived at the hotel on the Friday night, and the next morning many of them went off to Brockholes with their children while I was getting my hair done and generally being pampered ahead of the ceremony and reception on the Saturday.

My dad cut things fine by getting stuck in motorway traffic, and while sitting there, he realised with horror that he'd picked up the wrong suit and that it wasn't the one with his father of the bride speech in the pocket! Nevertheless, he pulled it off, ad-libbing his way through the crisis in his inimitable theatrical style to give a lovely, very funny speech.

Simon called me 'the love of my life' and talked about how happy he was that I'd agreed to marry him. His lovely father, Richard, welcomed me into the family, and then it was my turn. Determined to stand up and say something but overcome with nerves, I announced: 'You all know why you're here. Wow. Well, I finally found somebody I love a little bit more than myself.' Inexplicably daft, I know! Nothing like me at all!

After the speeches and the cake-cutting ceremony, more guests arrived for the evening disco, and the perfect day came to an end with us all sitting round eating bacon sandwiches in the early hours as a couple of guests played guitar and led us in a singalong. All that was left was for us to enjoy a small blessing at Rydal Chapel, just outside Ambleside, the following day. My sister Louise's vicar husband, also called Simon, conducted the lovely, warm service and made everybody laugh by saying: 'We knew it was serious with Simon when Jo talked about going camping!' True – camping was not my style at all!

Eventually, as with all good things, the celebrations had to end, but they ended on another high as, when we arrived back at our house, the neighbours had hung balloons and bunting announcing "Just Married" across the front door. What a different occasion to my first wedding! As my brother Tim said in the wedding book for guest messages: "You got your happy ending, Jo." I did. It's just as well though that I didn't know what heartache lay round the corner…

Fun in the Netherlands Em, Lauren, Freya

Simon indulging in his passion!

Langdale Chase Hotel revisiting fond memories of our big day

One of many trips with Simon, Dubai on route to Malaysia.

Langdale Chase Hotel, Windermere, The Big Day

Langdale Chase Hotel, Windermere, The Big Day - Photography courtesy of Ziggy

11

GOODBYE ZIGGY

I get the phone call one Saturday morning in May 2009 when I am living in the town of Sassenheim in the south of Holland with Simon and Em. Picking up my mobile with one hand, I sweep back the heavy maroon-velvet curtains in the living room with the other.

'Hello, Jo. It's Dad,' says the voice at the other end. 'I'm sorry, but I have got some sad news to tell you. Ziggy's been drowned.'

'What?' I manage to stutter.

'Ziggy's been drowned,' he says again.

There's a silence as I process his words. When I manage to speak to ask how he was found, Dad tells me that a dog walker spotted his body washed up on the beach at Ulverston, Cumbria, with no top on – just a pair of jeans.

'You need to be clear with me,' I demand.

'It doesn't make a difference to the outcome… He's died,' he adds.

At that moment, Emily walks into the room, and I know that I have to tell her the news. 'Emily, I'm really, really sorry, but Granddad has just phoned and said that Uncle Ziggy has died.' Throwing the toy she's holding onto the settee, she says: 'He promised me he was coming to visit me in Holland!' before running upstairs.

Suddenly, my tears came but, on automatic pilot, I pick up a basket of washing that I was about to hang on the clothesline and head outdoors with it. As I step outside, I see a dead sparrow on the bottom step leading down to the garden and the strangest, strongest feeling washes over me that this is an omen connected to Ziggy's death. I know it sounds crazy, but it was as if the dead bird was Ziggy. It's so weird.

The next thing I remember is Simon, who'd gone out for a haircut, coming through the front door, and Em, who was nine at the time, rushing to him, saying, 'Uncle Ziggy's dead!'

I don't know where all my tears came from that weekend – whole bucketloads of them. I had felt guilty about leaving Ziggy behind when we'd moved to Holland a year beforehand, but the relocation was because of Simon's job. He wanted to take up the opportunity being offered to him, and it was so important for his career that it was a no-brainer really. I knew what we had to do.

Besides, if I am completely honest, it was another chance to escape my past and reinvent myself. Another fresh start, and I always liked those. The further I moved away, the freer I always felt.

And life in Holland was good for all of us. We were living in a beautiful house with marble floors and big windows overlooking green fields and a canal. It was lovely to sit in the living room and just watch the boats sail past. We even had our own blue and white *sloep*, or small sailboat. Em had settled into international school well and she was thriving, despite being diagnosed with dyslexia, in that education system. She learnt to speak Dutch and in fact was better at it than I was. I went on a course and could get by asking for haircuts and things, but Em spoke the language fluently.

Although she missed her dad, my relationship with Doug had managed to get on a civil footing, and he'd been over to visit her. My mum and dad had been over to stay with us too. Em and I both had bikes, and we cycled everywhere together. I did a little bit of voluntary work at Em's school, and I discovered yoga and Pilates. It solved my back problems, and I became good friends with the lovely teacher, Jana. The two of us used to go for long walks on the beach together with her dog.

Simon was enjoying his new job, and Holland was good for me physically and mentally. Life was uncomplicated for once. But Ziggy had probably felt more at a loss after we left. Soon after Simon and I got married, Ziggy had moved up to Kendal and was living in a bedsit there. He'd been a regular visitor for Sunday dinner every week, and Simon had tried to help him find work, suggesting he got an HGV driving licence, which he did.

The last time I saw him, he'd driven an HGV lorry down our street, and I took a lovely photo of him and Em standing next to it. We were a little bit distant at that time; I wouldn't say we were in the best of places with our relationship. He was relatively sorted with a stable job and a regular wage coming in to pay his rent, but underneath he was still the same old Ziggy.

Before we left for Holland, I'd had a disturbing dream about Ziggy. I was in a queue at the top of a bank building, but suddenly, as I was moving forward, Ziggy came out of the building and announced: 'I'm not queuing anymore. I'm checking out.' In my dream, I responded by pleading: 'Ziggy, come back!'

At the time, I was undergoing counselling to help me come to terms with the problems of my past, and I can remember telling my counsellor about that strange dream. She told me firmly: 'If and when this is to happen, you are to know that this is not your fault.' Was it obvious to her that this ending was inevitable?

The news took time for me to process as I went about my normal chores quite mechanically, washing and ironing yet thinking all the time: 'Ziggy, my special brother that I'd shared my childhood with, is dead.' It just didn't feel real. I can only describe it as like losing a limb forever. It was such a physical feeling; it felt as if a part of my body – an arm or a leg – had been amputated. It still does. Totally knocked for six, I became irrationally angry with Mum and Dad and didn't want to be around my family, though I did stay at my sister Ro's house before the funeral on 3rd June at Harwood Park Crematorium.

Not wanting Em to be upset, I decided that I would go back to England alone for the funeral and Simon would stay at home to look after Em. I felt as if everything around me was crumbling, and things just got worse when I watched Ziggy being carried into a hearse in a beautiful oak coffin. I felt completely numb. Dad leant over and kissed me on the cheek, but all I could say was: 'That isn't Ziggy in the box.'

It was all a real shock, and it had triggered some strong feelings in me. Ziggy was the nearest thing I had to my own family, and without him, I felt like an outcast. I was angry, and I realised then that I had to deal with how I really felt about my adoptive family. Being around them was not a positive thing for me. All I wanted was to get back to Holland and Simon and Em as quickly as I could.

Ziggy's coffin arrived at the crematorium to the sound of Eva Cassidy's 'Fields of Gold'. I read a poem I'd written myself. There was a short Bible reading from the Gospel of Luke, followed by a recording of Pavarotti singing 'Ave Maria'.

Then it was time for the committal. It really was goodbye to Ziggy, who we discovered at a subsequent inquest into his death had died aged 37 as a result of drowning whilst intoxicated with alcohol. The button was pressed, the curtains closed, and Ziggy was on his way out of the world to the sound of Lou Reed's song 'Perfect Day'. I'd insisted on it being played because Ziggy had joked in the past about wanting it played at his own funeral.

Everybody says that's how we've got to go, but it seems so brutal when it's somebody you love. It's bizarre. Heartbroken, I filed out of the crematorium with the rest of the mourners. Not wanting to hang around, I went back to Holland the following day after spending another night at Ro's.

But it wasn't the same old Jo that was returning. I was a changed person – one with a burning need to face my past and find my own family. Especially – dare I hope – my birth mother. I had picked up the phone to the Thomas Coram Foundation once before at the age of 18 to find out what they could tell me, but I'd never followed it through. This time, I was more determined. Whatever the outcome, I was going into that emotional tunnel head-first. Once and for all.

Brother (Ziggy) & Sister moment - Wedding Morning, no jitters here!

Ziggy - Happy Days

Much Loved Uncle Ziggy, with Em, Lauren & Freya

12

HELLO ISABELLE

The new email that's landed in my inbox terrifies and excites me at the same time. It's from Ariel Bruce, a social worker who specialises in tracing people affected by adoption. For the last few weeks, she's been trying to track down my birth mother. Does this latest message mean she's found her?

There's only one way to find out, and that's to open the email. On doing so, an amazing sense of relief washes over me, and all I can think is: 'Wow! It's not too late.'

Triggered into action by Ziggy's death, I had phoned the Thomas Coram Foundation and spoken to Jane Greenwood, a senior adoption social worker there. After listening to my plea for help, she informed me that the good news was they still had all my records. She advised me to make an appointment to visit her and that she would go through them with me then. Good news indeed!

My adoptive mum kindly insisted on accompanying me, and as soon as I could, I flew back to London for the meeting on 24th August 2009. Mum didn't come into the room with me; there was just me and Jane, who sympathetically and professionally went through my story with me before handing me a print-out of my records along with handwritten notes from my birth mother.

As I struggled to stay composed, I learnt that I was born on 7th February 1969, at Paddington General Hospital, weighing 7lb 10z. My mother, Isabelle Byrne, delivered me normally and named me Anita Amar Byrne. She came from Scotland, where her father, Patrick, who was of Irish descent and a staunch Roman Catholic, was a bookmaker. His wife, Annie, was a mother of 12 and a housewife who'd been under pressure at home, which was not a particularly happy one.

Isabelle's childhood had been overshadowed by Patrick's rigid and stern beliefs, though she respected her very intelligent mother. After leaving school at 15, Isabelle had worked in an office and a chemist's shop before moving to London to work as a domestic in hotels almost three years before I was born.

It was there that she met my birth father, Kartar Singh, who was 26 when I was born. He'd travelled from Malaysia, where he'd been a teacher, to study law and become a barrister at Lincoln's Inn. Although no longer practising, he was a Sikh. Little was recorded about his family other than the fact his father worked in the military police, and he had one sister and two brothers.

Kartar and Isabelle had been in a relationship for some time and, infatuated with him, Isabelle had never doubted that he would marry her. It came as a shock to her on discovering she was pregnant that he wanted to have the baby – me! – adopted. Facing his final exams and living on a student grant, he felt he was in no position to take on the responsibility of marriage and a child, and Isabelle felt persuaded into having me adopted.

Three months before I was born, Isabelle saw Miss Czaczinsky, the medical social worker at Paddington, to make the necessary arrangements. Anxious and distressed, she told her she was going to Canada for a year to stay with her sister and then hopefully return to Kartar when he'd finished his studies.

Three days after my birth, Isabelle saw Miss Czaczinsky again and, as she breastfed me, she told her that she'd changed her mind about adoption as she couldn't bear to be parted from me. She hadn't yet told Kartar though…

Another three days later, aged just six days old, I went to live with a temporary foster mother while Isabelle sorted out plans to keep me and bring me up on her own. I knew it! Deep down in my bones, I always knew that my mum was strong and that she wanted to keep me.

'Isabelle very much wanted to keep you and asked for help to do so,' Jane reassured me. Just how much she wanted to keep me was then revealed in more detail as I learnt the heart-wrenching details of her agony in letting me go.

Although Isabelle hoped that Kartar would change his mind when I was born, it became evident that he wouldn't and, gradually, she saw less of him, realising he wasn't someone she wanted to marry. She also realised that she would have little support from her family. As such, an application was made to Coram, who offered help to unmarried mothers by placing their babies in the nursery until they were able to provide secure homes themselves. The governors agreed to help Isabelle, and aged just five weeks old, I moved into the small nursery there.

Isabelle travelled on the taxi journey there with me, and it was noted by the social worker there, Miss Rees-Hogg, that on the journey my mum was "almost entranced" by me and seemed delighted to be with me. Later in the day though, when signing the admission statement, she became upset.

Miss Rees-Hogg describes my mum as seemingly a very genuine person who could be confused and anxious. "She is a serious girl who has been greatly shocked by her experiences during the past year," she wrote. I was flatteringly described as "a bright, attractive baby, most energetic and forward for her age." That last bit struck another chord. Maybe if things had been different, I wouldn't have struggled at school or played the classroom clown. My life could have been entirely different.

Despite my mother being raised a Roman Catholic, she had me baptised into the Church of England on 27th March 1969 when I was seven weeks old. My grandmother, Isabelle's mother, had sent a white dress for the occasion, which had delighted Isabelle, who mentioned in her handwritten note that she had washed it for the occasion.

There was so much information to take in, but it is heart-warming and heart-breaking at the same time to know for certain how much she wanted to keep me. She visited me frequently at the home and had even persuaded Kartar to visit in the forlorn hope that he would change his mind. Obviously, he didn't.

All the time, she continued to make plans and maintained contact with Miss Rees-Hogg. She moved to a bedsit and changed her job to work until the early hours at a nightclub, which she was at pains to point out was respectable. After her sister Kathleen's marriage failed in Canada, she returned to Scotland, and Isabelle hoped that she'd move to London to share a flat with her and help look after me.

Obviously tormented, by June 1969, she realised that I needed a stable home and told Miss Rees-Hogg that, on balance, adoption would be best for me. Coram didn't place children directly for adoption at that time, so I was placed for adoption with the National Children Adoption Association. But just over a month later, at the end of July 1969, she withdrew her application as she couldn't face being parted from me.

All this to-ing and fro-ing – she's keeping me, she's keeping me not – I could just picture the scene in my head of her in her bedsit handing me over and then drawing me back. That image is still with me today. Despite having no plan, she was determined to provide a home for me herself and raise me alone. But realistically, how could she?

By January 1970 though, Coram were increasingly concerned about my future as I needed to join a family within a timescale that would not be emotionally harmful to me. Isabelle reported that her sister had moved to London. They'd found temporary accommodation and planned to look for permanent accommodation that would be a suitable home for me. But then, their father became ill, and Kathleen returned to Scotland to help her mother care for him.

Unhappy and anxious, Isabelle had changed jobs and was finding life difficult. Without money or family help, she began to realise how hard it would be to raise me. And when, a month later in February 1970, she was asked to make a firm decision, she agreed to have me adopted. After thinking long and hard about my future, she realised it was the only way to give me the security I needed and asked that I be placed with a stable, loving family. After making such a traumatic decision, she found it too painful to visit me in the home again, but she continued seeing her social worker.

When she went to Coram to sign the consent forms on 9th April 1970, she brought in a set of 12 photographs of me to keep, and she also sent a few pounds she could barely spare for my future. After I was placed for adoption with the Williams family, Isabelle returned to Coram on 23rd April 1970 to spend one last day and night with me before I moved to live with my new family. Afterwards, she continued to be informed about how I was settling in, but the last time Miss Rees-Hogg saw her, she was in her bedsit planning to travel to Canada.

So, there I had it. That was my story heard properly for the first time aged 40. It was all news to me. All those years without knowing. I sobbed and sobbed and then, still stunned by my discoveries, I flew back to Holland and tried to process it all.

Seeing me undergo an emotional breakdown of sorts, Simon asked me if I wanted to take things a step further and try to trace Isabelle. I thought about it and firmly decided that, yes, I did.

Simon isn't one to let the grass grow under his feet, and once a decision has been made, he makes it happen. He also has a knack for finding the right person for the right job, and after doing some research online, he hired Ariel.

Within no time at all, she had new information for us. The detailed content in the email report was formal and to the point. A woman of the same name and date of birth as my biological mother was living in Coatbridge, Glasgow, next door to her twin sister, Kathleen. A mobile phone number believed to be Kathleen's was included along with the address. But there was also a warning that although this information was sound, it was untested. Although it was unlikely that it was incorrect, there was that possibility.

In my head, I had been preparing myself for the fact that my action might have come too late and that my mother was already dead. But in my heart, I truly believed that she wanted me to get in touch with her…

For some reason, I understood that she couldn't come looking for me because she'd given me up, and when you make a decision like that, it's for good. There's no going back on it. That's my own ethos. I would probably have done the same myself.

At this point, all I wanted to do was pick up the phone and make the call, but to be honest, I wimped out and handed that job over to Simon. On tenterhooks, I stood by his side in the bedroom of our beautiful Dutch home as he dialled the number. After a couple of rings, it was picked up by a woman with a Glaswegian accent. Explaining who he was, Simon used the name I was born with and said: 'I'm here with Anita.'

I've absolutely no idea why, but she asked if I was a nurse before going on to tell him that she was on a bus on the way to bingo. Then, crucially, she added that Isabelle was at home. And all I could think was that she was alive! My mother was still alive!

'Can you phone back when I'm with her?' Kathleen asked Simon.

We didn't need asking twice, and after her bingo session, it was my turn to pick up the phone and speak to Kathleen, who told me: 'It's so good to hear from you. We've always wondered how you are. Isabelle is always wondering about you, talking about you… '

This initial reaction couldn't have been nicer, and I was left thinking why on earth didn't I do this earlier?

Kathleen wanted to know what my name was now, and we chatted a little before she handed me over to Isabelle.

'Hello,' came the small, wary, Scottish voice. The poor woman didn't know what to expect. It didn't cross my mind to call her 'Mum', and I found myself saying: 'Hello, Isabelle. This is Jo. Can you hear me okay?' Learning that she could, I gushed: 'I want you to know that I am okay and that I have never blamed you for what happened. I know the story, and I want you to know that I am all right.'

Bizarrely, she replied: 'Okay, Mrs Patel.' It felt a bit off, and she followed it up with other muddled comments that weren't good either. At that point, Kathleen took the phone from her and very apologetically told me: 'I am so sorry. Isabelle is okay. She's just had a wee whisky.'

Her words didn't make sense, and it wasn't very nice, but to be fair, I think she was in shock when she heard my voice, and she didn't know how to react. And I suppose that if she had been all lovely with me, it would have been even more devastating to have missed out on her mothering all these years.

Nevertheless, hearing this gave me a bit of an insight into the person she really was – not a princess after all, or even Lorraine Kelly, who I'd once looked at on TV and wondered if she could be my mum? (Impossible I know, logically, given the age difference alone, but that's how you think when you're adopted.)

After promising Kathleen that I would send her a photograph of me and Simon getting married, I came off the phone with a strong sense of a woman in huge pain that I had no real connection to. Maybe you expect an earth-shattering moment in your dreams, but this is what happens in real life. Doing as I had promised, I posted the photograph and left it a week before I phoned Kathleen to check that she'd received it okay. One more shock awaited.

'Oh, I am so glad you have phoned,' she said. 'I am so sorry, but Isabelle died in my arms last night.' Just as I found her, I lost her before even getting the chance to meet her.

Isabelle (Ida) - Where does the glamorous pose come from, Daughter like mother?

KATHLEEN   IDA

Isabelle (Ida) with twin sister Kathleen

Isabelle (Ida) - On her wedding day

13

DUBLIN DAYS

Now knowing that my grandfather was of Irish descent, I have no hesitation in agreeing to move to Dublin when Simon's company want to move him from Holland. Just how many fresh starts did a girl like me need?

After all the shock of finding my mother and immediately losing her, I am ready to move on again. The missing piece of the jigsaw is finally complete. There was nothing wonderful about my longed-for 'reunion', so I could tick that box in my mind and go forward.

I'd decided not to go to Isabelle's funeral. I was absolutely exhausted by all the trauma, and I didn't want all the attention from a family I'd never met and didn't know. I wasn't ready for it. I would like to have had the chance to meet her properly at least once, but I am grateful that I got the chance to speak to her and tell her what I wanted to tell her before she died of a burst ulcer (on our second wedding anniversary coincidentally).

Strangely, I wanted her to feel okay about giving me up, because I knew it wasn't a decision she'd taken lightly. And at the end of the day, what choice did she have in her circumstances? While collecting

Em from school, I told her the story very matter-of-factly. I wrote to Kathleen to tell her of my decision not to attend the funeral, and I wrote to Ariel Bruce thanking her for her professional help and telling her that the experience had been positive but that there'd been no emotional connection, which just about summed it up. All done and dusted.

Out of the blue, before Isabelle was even buried, I received a phone call from another stranger that left me taken aback once more. The nervous female voice at the other end said: 'Hello, is that Jo? I hope it's okay, but Auntie Kathleen gave me your number.' It soon became clear that this was my half-sister, Bonnie.

As well as the information about my birth mother and her sister, Ariel's report had contained detailed official information about other family members. This included birth, marriage and death details about Isabelle's parents, Patrick and Annie, and the names and dates of birth of all her 12 siblings – Mary, Bridget, Thomas, Patricia, Agnes, Alexander, Kathleen, Christopher, Annie, John, Patrick and Jane.

Even closer to home, it was also revealed that after giving me up for adoption, my birth mother had gone on to marry Fook Cheong Poon, described as a 28-year-old student. The marriage didn't last, and Isabelle reverted to her maiden name of Byrne. However, the marriage did produce two children – Robin Andrew and Bonnie Louise. Isabelle had also given birth to another child, Christopher James, whose father was listed as unknown. I had three half-siblings! And here on the other end of a telephone line was my half-sister Bonnie…

Though taken aback by the call, I can honestly say that I didn't consciously feel bitter or jealous that Isabelle had kept three other children when she'd given me up. I was just glad that she'd gone on to have other babies when she was in a position to keep them.

Bonnie sounded friendly enough, and I came off the phone after arranging to meet up with her in a big old-fashioned pub near King's Cross Station in autumn before we moved to Dublin. Sitting opposite each other, Bonnie nursing a brandy and me a glass of wine, felt surreal. It was like looking at a younger version of myself (she's nine years younger than me), even though we had different fathers. But I think it was her mannerisms that took me by surprise. Just like me, she talked at a hundred miles an hour, even though I can't remember what we actually talked about.

After a couple of hours, we left the pub and said our goodbyes, but at the ticket barrier at King's Cross, I turned round at exactly the same time as Bonnie did to give her a final wave. In that moment, I was completely overwhelmed. Was this the emotional connection I craved that was missing with my mother?

We'd already arranged to stay in touch by phone, so I headed over to my adoptive parents' house to spend the night there before heading back to Holland. Over dinner, I talked to them honestly about finding my mother and my meeting with Bonnie. To be honest, I don't think they really knew how to deal with it. I can only remember Dad being very quiet, which wasn't like him.

A lot was going on with the impending move to Dublin, and I admit that I wasn't great at keeping in touch with Bonnie at that time, though she did later visit us in Dublin. I was more concerned with settling Em, who'd cried when we told her we were moving countries again and that she had to leave her school and all her friends. It was another new beginning for her too.

Landing in the south of the city at Foxrock near Leopardstown, famous for its racecourse, we moved into a lovely modern detached house that Simon's company had rented for us in Brighton Square. Instantly, I felt at home in Dublin. I loved everything about this lively city, its rich culture and its warm, friendly people who you could rely on to 'tell it as it is'. The legendary 'craic' suited me just fine as did their great sayings. My favourite was always: 'You don't know until you know.' True enough.

I spent the first 18 months pottering about, but then I got a bike and went along to a local gym, Westwood Club. I loved the welcoming atmosphere there and, instinctively, I had a feeling that I would work there. I think Simon thought I was nuts when I told him! Even though I'd been a good runner at school, I am not really sporty at all. In fact, I am quite lazy, so I like to think that Pilates chose me. In Holland, my instructor, Jana, had briefly mentioned that I should work with her, and Robyn, my new instructor at Westwood, said the same thing a couple of times.

Although Robyn was 20 years younger than me, the two of us became quite friendly and had lunch together on occasion. To shut her up really, I ended up agreeing and signed myself up for a training course. After several weekends, I was a qualified instructor. I was even offered a job by the woman who had trained me. I hadn't really thought too much about what I would do afterwards, and knowing me, left to my own devices I'd have probably put the certificate away in a drawer and forgotten about it rather than put it to good use.

Simon, Em and I were due to go away on holiday, and I was really stressed about what to do. When we returned, the decision was almost made for me. Walking into the gym, Robyn and the manager, Andy, were chatting in the reception area and beckoned me over. Explaining that Robyn was leaving to go to Australia, Andy told me that she had recommended me for her job.

'What?' I replied, astonished and a bit overwhelmed. I made up every excuse not to do it, and beneath it all was my old fear that I wasn't good enough and would soon be found out. I was reassured by a number of other women in the class who knew me and wanted me to take over, so I started doing three classes a week. Pouring my adrenaline into something I liked doing and was actually quite good at, life was good again.

Em had settled in Dublin eventually, and we had a great time socially, enjoying meals and drinks out with Simon's colleagues, and the shopping was great.

Then, my adoptive dad became very ill, and it was clear that he didn't have long left to live. He'd been admitted to Addenbrooke's Hospital in Cambridge early in 2012 with pneumonia, and soon I was heading over there to meet up with Mum and say my goodbyes.

On arrival at the hospital, a doctor guided us into a side room and told us that at some point we would have to prepare to let him go. I remained strong despite knowing that this would be the last time I would see him and headed for his bedside.

On seeing me, he looked up at me and said: 'We did our best, Jo.'

I leant over, kissed him on the forehead and said: 'Dad, all these years you've spent with your faith… you have to believe now that you are going to be in that good place.' Yet, turning to simply say, 'Bye, Dad,' as I left his room for the last time, I just felt numb. Mum thanked me for my words, saying: 'You are so good at these things.' But while I may have been appearing calm on the surface, my feelings towards him were quite bittersweet.

Days later, when I was back in Dublin, I received the news in a phone call from my brother Tim that my father had died of pneumonia aged 85 and that he was still clutching a wooden cross in his hand at the end.

As with my birth mother, I took the decision not to attend his funeral. Once again, I felt overwhelmed with mixed emotions. I'd had so many difficulties with this man over the years, yet he'd always told me that I was special, and there are all those happy memories too – like the Christmases at Hadley Wood when Mum and Dad would set the alarm for 6am, and as soon as it rang, we'd all run downstairs to open our red corduroy stockings. There was always the smell of a pine Christmas tree in the air. It was quite magical really.

The added practical problem of Simon not being around to take care of Emily was also a factor in not attending the funeral. To be honest, I was glad of the geographical distance between Ireland and England. Besides, I had said my own private goodbyes. Later, I met up with my dad's sister-in-law, my aunt Anne, when she was visiting Dublin, and she told me that a white butterfly had flown off Dad's coffin at the funeral. If you believe in these things, spiritually, a white butterfly appearing at a funeral represents the deceased's soul fluttering into the afterlife in some cultures.

I also had a lovely dream about Dad soon after he died. In it, he was sitting in a garden, and around him there was a square full of beautiful flowers. It was enough to convince me to believe that he is in a nice place, wherever he is now.

On 25th February 2012, Simon, Em and I travelled over to Letchworth in Hertfordshire for a service of celebration and thanksgiving for my dad's life at St Paul's Church. I read a little speech, and we all sang 'To God Be the Glory' and 'Amazing Grace' while reflecting on his life, before leaving to the uplifting sound of a Scottish jig. At the church hall reception afterwards, we were encouraged to take a book that he had written about his life, one of his many ties and a jar of his famous chutney!

Afterwards, things carried on as normal in Dublin. My Pilates classes were becoming hugely successful, attracting up to 70 people at a time. Em completed her schooling and began working in the telesales department for Virgin, which she was good at. Then, the next bombshell came from Simon in 2017, who confessed to missing the UK and wanting to move back to his native Kendal where he would be closer to his own daughters and where he planned to retire eventually. I wasn't so sure. I was enjoying my Pilates teaching, and after the first two years of living in a rented house, we'd bought our own home which we'd finally got how we wanted it to be. But if Simon really wanted to return to the UK, I didn't want to say no to him.

Em was adamant that she wasn't coming with us though. She liked her life in Dublin and, at 18, didn't want to up sticks again. She has always been confident and grown-up for her age, so it was with a heavy heart that we eventually agreed. We rented her a flat, settled her in, and with promises of regular visits to and fro on both sides, we left her behind – a different goodbye to the ones that have marked my life but just as difficult. This time, I was the one leaving my own baby, and she was legally an adult, but it was so hard. How on earth did my birth mum cope?

Climbing high with Simon - Carrauntoohil, Ireland

Jo Jo Pilates

14

LIVE, LAUGH, LOVE...

Stunned by what Em has just told me on the phone, I choose my words carefully. In my heart and in my head, I know that what I say next is important because she will remember it for the rest of her life. My response has to sound as joyous as it genuinely is.

It's just before Christmas 2019 when my mobile rings as I'm preparing for a trip to London with Simon. 'Mum, I really need to see you,' Em begins.

'Why?' I ask. After spending a year of living the Dublin life without us, she had, thankfully, followed us to Kendal, where we're living in a romantic old farmhouse in a picturesque hamlet surrounded by hills and sheep. Although she now lives in a rented flat across town with her lovely, hardworking partner, Dylan, and works full-time at a mobile phone store, we're hardly strangers.

'Don't worry. It's nothing bad,' she reassures me, and before she even goes on to say the words: 'I'm pregnant,' I already know. Instinctively, I also know that this must not and cannot be a negative experience for her.

She may be only 20 and unmarried – like my own birth mother was – but a pregnancy is an amazing thing, and I immediately tell her so. I don't think that she could quite believe my reaction, but it's the only one she's getting from me.

At 29 and pregnant with Em, I was scared stiff of telling my parents, and I never wanted her to feel like that. She has my full support, and she always will have. All I want is for her to be happy, and my way of dealing with things is to think: 'Okay, this is really happening. Now, what can I do to support Em? I could choose to be judgmental, but what good would that be?'

I remember telling my eldest brother, Roger, how I felt about it. 'It's wonderful news!' I say quite honestly. Nevertheless, it was a shock to me and to Simon, but he was pretty cool about it too when the news sunk in that we were actually going to be grandparents – I'll have another blood relative in the world! They're growing all the time!

Kathleen had continued to write regularly to me after Isabelle's death, and I had had a letter from her sister – another aunt called Janie – after Kathleen gave her my address. It was a lovely letter, and it contained some heart-warming details about Ida, which was the name she knew Isabelle by.

Ravenous for any information about her that I could find, I was immensely grateful. Janie wrote from her home in Cornwall and began by explaining that she was the youngest of her mother's 13 live-born children. After her home birth in 1957, her mother was dangerously ill with septicaemia. Janie was sent to live with a

paternal aunt, and it wasn't until the age of 14 that she saw Ida for
the first time. She wrote:

*I was looking out of our front window and saw a lady alight from
a car that had pulled up opposite. She was dressed immaculately
in a well-fitted, classy black coat; her hair was long, blonde,
silky and was neat underneath her fashionable, floppy black hat.
I remember actually exclaiming aloud: 'Oh, look, the Millers
opposite have a movie star visiting,' only to be informed that the
lady was my sister.*

*I was extremely excited that I had a sister who looked so
Hollywood cosmopolitan. I had of course by then known that I
had a sister called Ida and that she was Kathleen's twin. They
looked similar but not identical and were distinguishable.*

*The second time I met Ida was when she lived in Bayswater
in central London. I was about 15 years old then, and I got to
know her a little.*

*Although older than me by some years, she was still a little
girl really, trying to survive in a large metropolitan city and
struggling along to survive. This was when she told me about
your father, you and your adoption. She had drunk some wine
and was crying inconsolably. She explained about being deserted
and let down by the love of her life and how she had to give you
up. She told me she called you Anita. She told me that your father
was from overseas, studying to be a lawyer and that he was
terrified of his family finding out he had a relationship before
qualifications, etc.*

I tried to comfort her by telling her that you would hopefully be adopted into a secure and nurturing environment with parents who would provide you with everything they could.

However, even at my young age, I knew and recognised the depth of her sorrow and despair about your birth situation. She never got over that decision, and throughout the years I was in contact with her she didn't fail to mention your name.

When I left the confines of our village at a tender age, I made my way down south towards London and Essex. I headed to Ida's. She was married by then to Fook Cheong Poon and was expecting a baby. I lodged with them on many occasions as I came and went, working for my living. In fact, everyone who arrived down south from Scotland stayed at Ida's until they settled themselves independently. She was always there for us. Ida's became the second home until you found your own.

Jo, I have to tell you here that your mum was bipolar and suffered extremely badly with the effects of the dark depression that uncontrollably engulfed her. Even now, there is a huge stigma associated with depression, and back then I guess you can only imagine what it was like.

Although she had some nice times, and I saw her laughing at times too, she always had that melancholy look, and it never took long to surface. She used to try and find solace with drink, but it always made everything worse and, mixed with the medications, well, she didn't cope.

However, I have great memories of her on sunny days in Essex when we would go shopping together and stop off for lunch. She always had good taste in clothes, and with her light suntanned face, I can still see her now in my head, smiling and enjoying those times.

You have probably heard in the media that Marilyn Monroe was an ordinary-looking girl who you might pass in the street unless she was in her 'mode'. That is, she would invoke the persona of the movie star within her, and this mode would be noticed, would command attention and people would recognise her then. Well, I have to tell you that Ida had that strange gift of raising her 'auric profile'. It was astonishing to watch, and it would mesmerise anyone and everyone in the vicinity.

Her mind was sharp at times, and she could instantly read personalities at a glance. She saw right through to the other side. She enjoyed it when the family and friends came to stay as it lifted her spirits. She was lovely and happy at times, but I know she always struggled with the fact that she wasn't strong or mature enough to raise you herself.

I have to say that I found it utterly amazing that you managed to speak to her at that time in her last moments. It was meant to be on some level, and I am so happy for both of you that you did. I guess it reassured her, albeit in her latter days, that you were okay after all.

And there I have it – further proof that my mother wanted me and didn't give me up easily. And even though she might not have been a princess, she was a movie star – of sorts!

Janie goes on to explain more of the family background and the village she came from in that era. She describes the people living there as "quite secular, all white, mainly Christian and uneducated in the multicultural aspects of a global society. To have a child outside marriage at that time was a sin too far, and it was for this reason that Ida could not have returned there at that time to have you and mother you. It's all changed now – the world is a global village now – but back then, they would have, in their blind innocence, crucified you both so to type… "

It is heart-breaking stuff, and I can't help thinking in another time and another place how different things could have been. Janie adds details about how close Ida and Kathleen were, how much Kathleen misses her sister but also how very happy she was that we had contact.

Janie ends her letter by wishing me well and welcoming me to her home if I am ever visiting Cornwall. I haven't done so yet, but maybe I will someday.

I did meet my two half-brothers, Robin and Christopher, when I flew over to London from Dublin with Simon and Em for Bonnie's wedding. But I can't honestly say that I felt any real emotional connection to them or that I wanted to know any more about them. Em, who was actually a bridesmaid, remembers the whole situation as a bit odd and was very protective of me at the pub reception.

Soon after we arrived back in Kendal, I also met up with Kathleen. I'd travelled to Glasgow with Simon, who was meeting a business client in the city, and I caught the train out to Coatbridge, where we'd arranged to meet in a pub. It was a freezing cold, really snowy day, and I was feeling quite nervous, but I knew I had to do this, and I did wonder if it would be a bit like meeting my mum.

Bizarrely, I got talking to a nice man and woman who were fellow train passengers, and they were on their way to interview somebody with a story similar to mine. What are the chances of that happening? 'Good, good luck!' they kindly told me as we parted company.

Arriving in good time, I found the pub and went in to find the only other person in there was the cleaner. It was early morning! Sitting in a corner with a window behind me, I eventually turned to look outside and could see a petite woman aged 70-plus with frizzy brown hair. This had to be her!

She walked into the pub clutching a bag of bread to feed to the ducks and walked past me at first, which was hilarious! It was just like the sort of thing I'd do! She had a real presence about her and seemed happy to meet me.

Once the introductions were over, I bought her a coffee and we made conversation. I don't even recall most of what we said – it's such a blur. But I do remember her telling me that I looked like my aunt Janie and giving me a poncho that she wanted Em to have. That really struck me. Here was a woman who was giving me something, and yet she had nothing herself...

We were together there for an hour tops because she was going to bingo again that afternoon, which she was so excited about, and she needed to buy a sandwich from Tesco for her lunch first.

I can't honestly say it was the next best thing to meeting my mum. I don't think it fulfilled that need in me, but I was glad to have met her, and I never got a second chance to do it.

We stayed in touch by letter until I got a call from Bonnie to tell me that Kathleen had died. Though I was invited to the funeral, I declined. I didn't want to get caught up meeting all the family at once in such emotional circumstances; it would have been too much. Overwhelming.

So, I went back to my life in Kendal, where I carried on teaching my Jo-Jo Pilates classes face to face and eventually online. Then, on 10th August 2020, my whole world changed and became brighter when my beautiful granddaughter, Daisy May, was born into a locked-down world because of the COVID-19 outbreak. Poor Em hadn't had an easy pregnancy at all. She'd spent most of it stuck indoors at home until it was time to go to hospital in Barrow-in-Furness and be induced because of a few complications with her kidneys.

Although full of ideas about natural childbirth – Em especially wanted a water birth – that didn't happen as she was given a pill to induce her and speed up her baby's arrival.

After she phoned to promise that she would call me back later when her baby had arrived, I headed for the spare bed in the back room. There was no point in Simon having a sleepless night as well as me.

I got my first glimpse of Daisy May when she was just minutes old lying next to her mum. Dylan had actually phoned with the news and sent that first photo to my mobile. It was all so emotional!

Em looked terrified and happy at the same time. I just felt so proud of her – really proud. She was only young herself. She's still my little girl with the freckles on her nose, and she'd given birth. She did it!

Simon and I met our new granddaughter in person at their home the following day. Weighing exactly 7lb with big blue eyes and fair hair, she looked a lot like her mum. Bursting with pride, I held my baby's baby. It felt so surreal, and she was so tiny.

Mum came to visit, followed by Bonnie, who has no children, and stayed for several days to provide additional practical help. Bonnie and Em had always clicked – it was uncanny really.

A year on, Em still phones me every day to update me when I am not with them both or on grandma duty. Daisy May is a bright shining light, but sometimes I do think about the girl in the purple dress and how she felt at that same age… Daisy May knows my voice and eagerly puts her arms out to come to me. It's an amazing feeling. Such a joy!

When you have a grandchild, it also makes you aware of your own mortality, and it's making me want to grab what's left of life. I want my daughter and granddaughter to grab life too, and I have already told Em that when I die (hopefully not for a long time!), I want her to be sad for a day or two and then make a good thing of it. Take the good memories of me and let her own life story evolve. My own's evolving all the time.

Finally, 12 whole years since Ziggy's death, I plucked up the courage to visit the Ulverston beach where he was found. His girlfriend at the time, Fuj, directed me to the exact location where the local dog walker found him, three days after his passing early in the morning.

Simon, my sister Louise and her husband Simon, came with us. As the five of us sat on the sloping old railway banking stones overlooking the sandy runnel where Ziggy had lain, we remembered him fondly. Louise and Simon, who are both vicars, led prayers and back came the tears and the familiar sinking feeling of loss and pain in the pit of my stomach.

Simon agreed with me that the stone I was sitting on was the perfect place for Ziggy to have pondered his life as he enjoyed the sunshine. Looking down at the base of it, I suddenly spotted a twig in the shape of a cross, which I took as a comforting symbol. Picking it up to take home with me, I knew that I never wanted to be parted from it.

Not for the first time, I allowed myself to question whether he really did take his own life. I've never really believed that he did and always felt his sudden death was just a tragic accident. But I've just accepted it all these years. Actually being there though allowed me to voice my true feelings out loud. I could almost see Ziggy sitting on that rock, folding his clothes and leaving them there along with a full bottle of tequila to follow the one he'd just downed, and going for a cooling dip. I also saw for myself just how fast the tide comes in there on that particular stretch of coastline.

Was this another Russian roulette wheel that Ziggy was on, testing whether he'd live or die? Or was he so sloshed with alcohol that he got caught out? Only God knows, but I know what I believe. Yes, it was death by drowning and alcohol as the death certificate says, but I believe that this time his game was up and that he drowned accidentally, not deliberately.

Though I was unsettled for days afterwards, it was also quite a healing process. Em cried when I told her the details of our visit. Like me, she feels that she can cope better if it was an accident. It makes the pain of suicide more bearable, and there's a new acceptance of events.

Quite literally, I am now finally moving on. Simon and I have now sold our farmhouse home and are moving into a newer property across town to be closer to Daisy May, Em and Dylan. I love being part of their lives, and I am thankful for that.

I will always be grateful to Simon too. He's always listened to me and been a calming influence. We complement each other well. He's a very practical, logical doer, while I am the intuitive, emotional, sensitive one with a few complexities that make life fun and colourful for us at times! He could see where I was coming from in 2004, and he saw that his job was to nurture and love me. He has showered me with love.

Simon and Em are my best friends, but I also treasure my relationship with my stepdaughters, Freya and Lauren, who've long grown out of those Monsoon dresses I sold them! I love their sheer resilience and thirst for enjoying life.

My adorable Daisy May has an extra special place in my life. When I spend time with her, I am kept fully in the moment, and any worries or concerns that I have simply melt away.

I know it's become a bit overused as it's on everything from posters to mugs, but there's a lot to be said for the phrase 'Live,

Laugh, Love'. When I think about it, it was summed up by my auntie Kathleen. Being quite a simple soul myself, I loved her humbleness. There was something so vibrant about the way she lived and just accepted her lot in life. There's a lot to be said for that, and I strive to do the same. Live. Laugh. Love.

Bonnie's wedding day

best mama in
the world x

All grown up!

15

AND ALWAYS HOPE

J ust when I'm adding the finishing touches to my own adoption story in 2021, a prominent item flashes up on BBC News at Ten and makes me sit up.

Shockingly, up to 250,000 women in Britain were coerced into handing over their babies for adoption in the 1950s, 60s and 70s because they were unmarried. Hundreds of them are calling on the Prime Minister to issue a government apology for forced adoptions, as Australia did in 2013.

Many of the women never had more children and say the loss caused them a lifetime of grief. In interviews with some of the women themselves, they describe being an unmarried mother as 'deeply humiliating' and 'a fate worse than death'.

Lawyers examining the birth mothers' cases between 1945 and 1975 – my own era and before changes in adoption law were made – say around 500,000 babies were adopted in Britain, just like me. Most of those mothers were under 24 and unmarried, just like my mum. I wasn't alone, and neither was she.

The lawyers' research suggests that about half of those women faced sustained pressure to give up their babies from professionals, including doctors, midwives, workers in mother-and-baby homes and adoption staff in religious and council-run homes. One woman recalls that she wasn't given pain relief during labour and was told by the midwife: 'You'll remember this so you won't be wicked again.'

It's inhumane and incredibly disturbing to watch. Who knows what agony my own mother went through? Adopted children like me are also interviewed, and it's a surprise to hear them echo my own struggles and feelings. I am perfectly normal to feel the way I do! These feelings are natural and caused by being adopted; they're the lasting impact of adoption.

As one woman adopted at birth in 1963 says: 'It's like a piece of me is missing.' How many times have I said that very phrase throughout my life?

Of course, there is still one large piece of my own jigsaw puzzle missing. I still don't know anything about my birth father, Kartar Singh, or any of his family. When Simon was on a business trip to Asia several years ago, I did accompany him specifically so that I could go back to my roots and visit Malaysia, the country where half of me originates from. It proved to be a very poignant adventure, and I felt a strong sense of connection there.

Nevertheless, it didn't produce any long-lost paternal relatives. Neither did the letter I sent to the former home of my grandfather, Ranjii Singh, several months ago. Simon managed to get the address where Kartar's family are believed to have been living around the time of my birth after making enquiries at Lincoln's Inn, one of the four inns of court where barristers in England and Wales belong and where they are called to the Bar. They also confirmed that Kartar Singh, aged 26, attended training there, but he never actually completed it. So, ultimately, I was rejected by my own father for no good reason whatsoever. It was all for nothing. Oh, irony of ironies.

Nevertheless, I sent out an appeal to this new address for any information, big or small, along with two pictures of the girl in the purple dress.

It was promptly returned, unopened, to me with the words "No Such Person" written by hand on the envelope. Disappointing? Yes. The end of my story? I hope not. If I have learned anything on this journey, it's that you should never give up hope about who's out there and whether they'll ever turn up to complete the family puzzle. To anyone who's ever been adopted, like me, I would advise the same. Always, always carry hope.

The Williams Clan (the women!)

The Williams Clan (the men!)

Em & Daisy May happy days

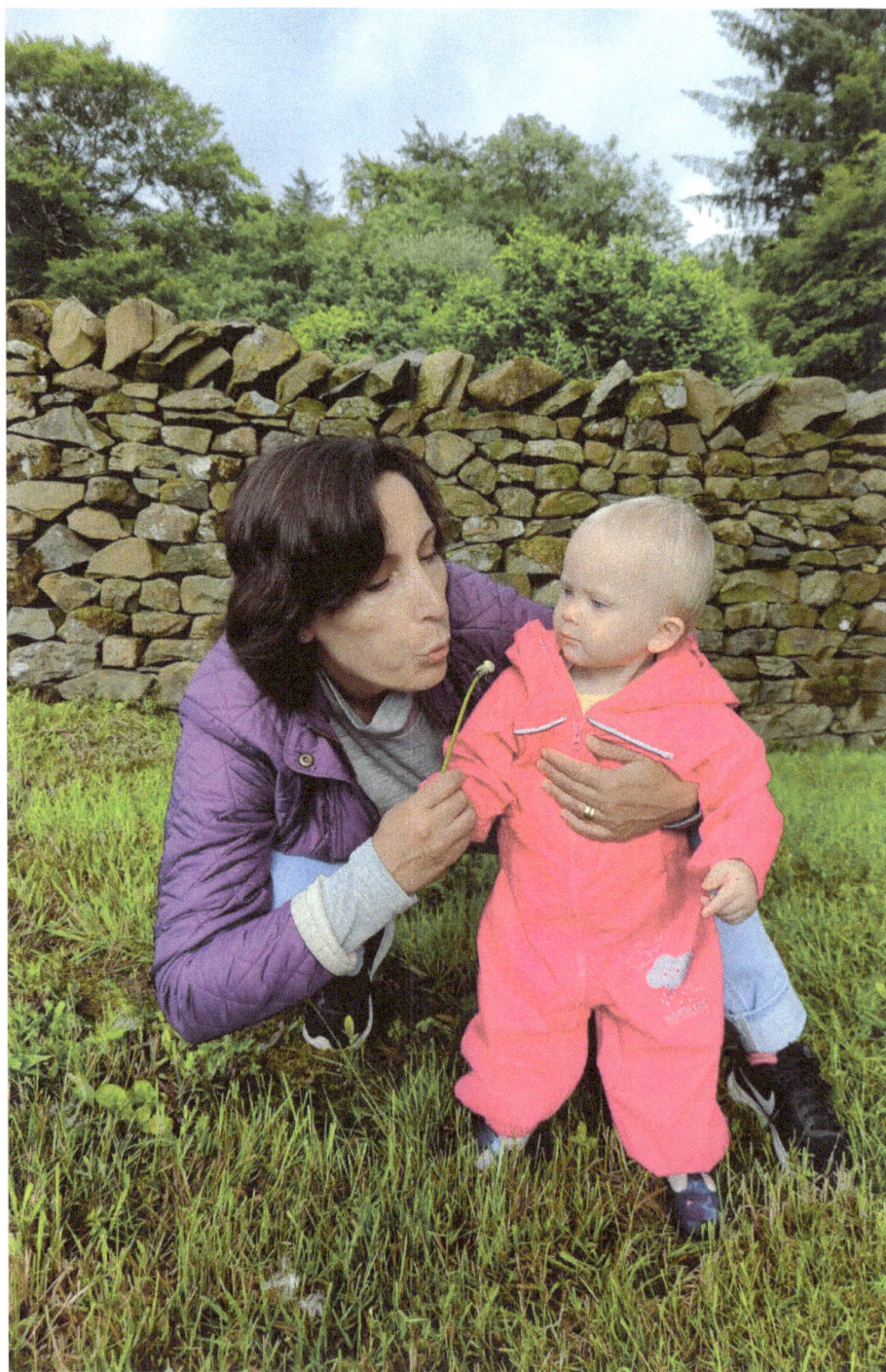

Wishes in the meadow with Daisy May

Four generations Mum (Di), Me (Jo), Daughter (Em) and Grandaughter (Daisy May)

Happy, Happy Days swinging with Daisy May

StoryTerrace

Milton Keynes UK
Ingram Content Group UK Ltd.
UKHW021544080424
440701UK00002B/17

9 781739 850616